Transactions
of the
American Philosophical Society
Held at Philadelphia
For Promoting Useful Knowledge
Volume 89, Pt. 4

A Reluctant Author:
Cardinal Pole and his Manuscripts

THOMAS F. MAYER
Augustana College

American Philosophical Society
Independence Square ✷ Philadelphia
1999

Copyright © 1999 by the American Philosophical Society for its *Transactions* series. All rights reserved. Cover background photograph: page from Pole's *De summo pontifice*, Bibliothèque municipale de Douai, MS 922, vol. IV, p. 7.

ISBN: 0-87169-894-3
US ISSN: 0065-9736

Library of Congress Cataloging-in-Publication Data

Mayer, Thomas F. (Thomas Frederick), *1951-*
   A reluctant author: Cardinal Pole and his manuscripts / Thomas F. Mayer.
   p.cm. --(Transactions of the American Philosophical Society, ISSN 0065-9736 ; v. 89, pt. 4)
   Includes bibliographical references and index.
   ISBN 0-87169-894-3 (pbk.)
   1. Pole, Reginald, 1500-1558--Manuscripts--Catalogs. I. Title. II. Series.

Z6616.P594 M39 1999
[DA317.8 .P6]
016.282'092--dc21

                                                                      99- 048301

Contents

Abbreviations iv
Short Titles iv
Introduction 1
Catalogue 42
Index 112

Abbreviations

Archives and Libraries

ASAS Bergamo, Biblioteca Civica "Angelo Mai," Archivio Stella in Archivio Silvestri

ACDFSO Archivio della Congregazione per la Dottrina della Fede, Sanctum officium

ASV Archivio Segreto Vaticano

ASVe Archivio di Stato, Venice

BAV Biblioteca Apostolica Vaticana

BCQ Brescia, Biblioteca Civica "Queriniana"

BNM Venice, Biblioteca Nazionale Marciana

BNN Naples, Biblioteca Nazionale "Vittorio Emmanuele III"

BPP Parma, Biblioteca Palatina

CCCC Corpus Christi College, Cambridge, Parker Library

LPL London, Lambeth Palace Library

PBN Paris, Bibliothèque Nationale

PRO London, Public Record Office

Short Titles

Beccadelli Ludovico Beccadelli, "Vita del cardinale Reginaldo Polo," in G. B. Morandi, ed., *Monumenti di varia letter-atura*, two vols. (Bologna: Istituto per le scienze, 1797-1804, 2, pp. 277-333.

Bonelli Giuseppe Bonelli, "Un archivio privato del Cinque-cento: Le Carte Stella," *Archivio storico Lombardo*, 34 (1907): pp. 332-86.

C. H. Cooper and Thompson Cooper, *Athenae Cantabrigienses*, two vols. (Cambridge: Deighton and Bell, 1858-61), 1, p. 185.

De Frede Carlo De Frede, *La restaurazione cattolica in Inghilterra sotto Maria Tudor nel carteggio di Girolamo Seripando* (Naples: Libreria scientifica, 1971).

Abbreviations

CRP Thomas F. Mayer, ed., *A Calendar of the Correspondence of Reginald Pole* (forthcoming).

CSPDom rev. C. S. Knighton, ed., *Calendar of State Papers Mary I*, revised edition (London: HMSO, 1998).

CSPV Rawdon Brown, ed., *Calendar of State Papers and Manuscripts, Relating to English Affairs in the Archives and Collections of Venice*, nine vols. (London: Longman, et al., 1864-98).

CT 1, *Concilii Tridentini Actorum Pars Prima*, ed. Stephan Ehses (Freiburg: Herder, 1904); 2, *Diariorum Pars Secunda*, ed. Sebastian Merkle (Freiburg: Herder, 1911); 8, *Actorum Pars Quinta*, ed. Stephan Ehses (Freiburg: Herder, 1919); 12, *Diariorum Actorum Epistularum Tractatuum nova collectio* (Freiburg: Herder, 1929).

DBI A. M. Ghisalberti, ed, *Dizionario biografico degli italiani* (Rome: Istituto dell' Enciclopedia italiana, 1960-).

Dodd Charles Dodd, pseudonym of Hugh Tootell, *The Church History of England from the Year 1500 to the Year 1688, Chiefly with Regard to Catholicks*, 1 (Brussels [but Wolver- hampton] : no publisher, 1737), pp. 479-80.

ERP Angelo Maria Querini, ed., *Epistolarum Reginaldi Poli*, five vols. (Brescia: Rizzardi, 1744-57).

Fragnito, "Censura" Gigliola Fragnito, "Aspetti della censura ecclesiastica nell' Europa della controriforma: l'edizione parigina delle opere di Gasparo Contarini," *Rivista di storia e letteratura religiosa*, 21 (1985), pp. 3-48.

Freher Paulus Freher, *Theatrum virorum eruditione singulari clarorum* (Nürnberg: J. Hofmann, 1688), p. 30.

Ghilini Girolamo Ghilini, *Teatro d'huomini letterati* (Venice: Guerigli, 1647), p. 204.

Klaiber Wilbirgis Klaiber, *Katholische Kontroverstheologen und Reformer des 16. Jahrhunderts. Ein Werkverzeichnis* (Münster: Aschendorff, 1978; Reformationsgeschichtliche Studien und Texten, 116).

L&P J. S. Brewer, James Gairdner and R. H. Brodie, eds., *Letters and Papers, Foreign and Domestic of the Reign of Henry VIII*, twenty-nine vols. (London: HMSO, 1862-1932).

Lutz Heinrich Lutz, ed., *Nuntiaturberichte aus Deutschland. Erste Abteilung 1533-1559*, 15, *Friedenslegation des Reginald Pole zu Kaiser Karl V. und König Heinrich II. (1553-1556)* (Tübingen: Niemeyer, 1981).

Nomenclator SRE Cardinalium (Tolosae [Toulouse?]: Dominicum de la Case, 1614), p. 132.

Mansi Giovanni Domenico Mansi, ed., *Sacrorum conciliorum nova et amplissima collectio*, fifty-four vols. (Florence: Antonio Zatta, 1759-1927).

Pagano-Ranieri Sergio M. Pagano and Concetta Ranieri, eds., *Nuovi documenti su Vittoria Colonna e Reginald Pole* (Vatican City: Archivio vaticano, 1989; Collectanea Archivi Vaticani, 24).

Pitts John Pitts, *De illustris Angliae scriptoribus* in *Relationum historicarum de rebus Anglicis*, 1 (Paris: Rolin Thierry and Sebastian Cramory, 1619), pp. 757-59.

Possevino Antonio Possevino, *Apparatus sacri*, four vols. (Venice: Society of Jesus in Venice, 1606), 3, p. 123.

Proc. Car. Giacomo Manzoni, ed., "Il Processo Carnesecchi," *Miscellanea di storia italiana*, 10 (1870): 189-573.

PM Massimo Firpo and Dario Marcatto, eds., *Il processo inquisitoriale del Cardinal Giovanni Morone*, six vols. (Rome: Istituto italiano per la storia dell'età moderna e contemporanea, 1981-95).

Rocaberti Juan Tomás Rocaberti, *Bibliotheca maxima pontificia*, twenty-one vols. (Rome: Giovanni Francesco Buagni, 1698), 18.

STC A. W. Pollard and G. R. Redgrave, eds., rev. W. A. Jackson and F. S. Ferguson and completed by K. F. Pantzer, *A Short-Title Catalogue of Books Printed in England, Scotland and Ireland and of English Books Printed Abroad before the Year 1640*, three vols. (London: The

Abbreviations

Bibliographical Society, 1976-91).

Tanner Thomas Tanner, *Bibliotheca britannico-hibernica: sive de scriptoribus qui in Anglia, Scotia, et Hibernia ad saeculi XVII initium floruerunt* (London: G. Bowyer, 1748; reprinted Tucson: Audax Press, 1963), pp. 602-3.

Torrigio Francesco Maria Torrigio, *De eminentissimis S.R.E. scriptoribus cardinalibus* (Rome: Stefano Paolinio, 1641), pp. 46-47.

Wood Anthony à Wood, *Athenae oxonienses*, ed. Philip Bliss, four vols. (London: F. C. and J. Rivington, et al., 1815; originally published in 1668), 1, cc. 292-3.

Editorial symbols

These apply either to the word immediately preceding or to everything following an asterisk in the line of text before the square brackets.

ab. above
ab. del. above deleted
aft. after
aft. del. after deleted
bel. below
del. deleted
mar. in margin
ov. over

Introduction

Cardinal Reginald Pole (1500-1558) left an abundance of manuscripts that have lacked an inventory and description. This monograph is intended to remedy that lack and perhaps contribute to a critical edition of some of his major works, especially *Pro ecclesiasticae unitatis defensione* (*De unitate*), "Apologia ad Carolum Quintum," *De summo pontifice*, *De sacramento*, a more complete version of *Discorso di pace*, and, the most difficult text, "De reformatione ecclesiae." In order to grasp the importance of such a project, a sketch of Pole's career and the significance of these works is in order.

Pole's Life and Works

Cousin of Henry VIII, cardinal, nearly successful candidate for pope, Archbishop of Canterbury, cultural conduit and leader of both the English and Italian Reformations, Pole was one of the most important international figures of the mid-sixteenth century.[1] As the first well-known anti-Machiavellian, he also plays a large part in the history of political thought. Pole's patronage of a generation of both English and Italian writers and his hand in directing the creation of a saintly Thomas More and John Fisher and their antitype the diabolical Henry VIII had a heavy impact on European historiography of the English Reformation.

As grandsons of the duke of Clarence, Pole and his oldest brother Henry Lord Montague posed a Yorkist threat to the new

---

[1] This summary is largely based on my *Reginald Pole, Prince and Prophet* (Cambridge University Press, forthcoming). My thanks to Francesco Cesareo, Thomas Freeman, Andrew Gow, Charles Knighton, Thomas McCoog, SJ, John Marmion, Richard Rex, Glyn Redworth, Sharon Strocchia, and the Interlibrary Loan staff of Augustana College for their help. Special thanks to Cardinal Josef Ratzinger and Monsig. Alberto Bovone for granting access to the ACDFSO, and to Monsig. Alejandro Cifres for his assistance in using it.

Tudor dynasty.[2] Nevertheless, Henry VII and even more Henry VIII restored Pole's family. Henry VIII made Pole's mother, Margaret, Countess of Salisbury, governess of Princess Mary and paid for Pole's education, first at Oxford (until 1521) and then in Padua (1521-26). There Pole very quickly met the dean of Paduan humanists, Pietro Bembo, and through him the papal datary, Gian Matteo Giberti, who would be one of Pole's most important mentors. His tutor, Niccolò Leonico Tomeo, was the first philosopher to propose restoring the Greek text of Aristotle, and Pole was on the fringes of the Aldine Galen edition. Until at least the early 1530s, Pole pursued his education as the king wished, by preparing himself to enter royal service. In 1529-30 he scored a major success when he directed the campaign to secure from the University of Paris a favorable opinion on Henry's divorce.[3] Yet Pole was not comfortable with that policy, and after giving Henry an extensive opinion on the dangers the divorce posed, left England in early 1532, but still in full royal favor. The story of his interview with Henry in which the king first offered Pole the Archbishopric of York in exchange for support of the divorce and then threatened to kill Pole when he refused the deal is almost certainly an invention. After a brief stop in Avignon and Carpentras where Pole met another important ally, Jacopo Sadoleto, he returned to Venice for the next four years.

In 1535, Pole faced a turning-point. The king demanded an unequivocal opinion on the divorce, and Pole responded with *De unitate* (catalogue no. 1), finished in early 1536. While it is far from the strongly papalist statement it has usually been considered, it forthrightly condemned Henry. It also reflected a religious conversion to an evangelical idea of the church and belief in justification by faith, making Pole one of the so-called *spirituali*. At the same time, Pole opened technically treasonous negotiations with the emperor. Henry did not know of these and

---

[2] For Montague, see my article in H. C. G. Matthew, ed., *The New Dictionary of National Biography* (Oxford: Oxford University Press, forthcoming). Hereafter *New DNB*.

[3] Thomas F. Mayer, "A Mission Worse than Death: Reginald Pole and the Parisian Theologians," *English Historical Review*, 103 (1988): 870-91.

Introduction

did not abandon Pole, although the book certainly angered him. When the Pilgrimage of Grace, a rebellion partly demanding restoration of traditional religion, erupted in October, Henry's anger deepened. Paul III's decision, at the suggestion of Pole's new patron Cardinal Gasparo Contarini, to make Pole a cardinal in December to replace the executed Fisher and then appoint him legate to aid the Pilgrims made things that much worse.[4] Pole spelled out the aims of his legation to the pope (catalogue no. 14), and Paul endorsed Pole's views and provided a great deal of finanical backing. Nevertheless, the legation did not accomplish much, largely because of imperial opposition to intervention in England, but it did convince Henry that Pole had to be dealt with. The king, however, had no more success than Pole.

Pole had become a man of consequence in Rome, in alliance with Contarini, and took part in the papal reform commission that issued the *Consilium de emendanda ecclesia* (catalogue no. 40) in 1538. Locating the root of the church's troubles in the pope's abuse of his power, its proposals would have disassembled the financial basis of papal monarchy. Thanks in part to Luther's mocking commentary as well as the opposition of curial traditionalists, the proposal remained a dead letter. Nevertheless, Pole was securely identified as a reformer.

In 1539 he had a second chance to move against Henry, once more as papal legate, entrusted to make peace between the king of France and the emperor, an effort designed to lead to action against England. Once again Pole failed, but this time he put his legation to good use by writing the "Apology" to Charles V, explaining what he had meant by appealing in *De unitate* to the people (that is, the nobility) against the king. Although Charles was unconvinced, the "Apology" is more important as the first sustained attack on Machiavelli, as well as the source of the image of Henry's chief minister Thomas Cromwell as an unscrupulous follower of Machiavelli, an opinion that dominated

---

[4] Thomas F. Mayer, "A Diet for Henry VIII: The Failure of Reginald Pole's 1537 Legation," *Journal of British Studies*, 26 (1987): 305-31 and "If Martyrs are Exchanged with Martyrs: the Kidnappings of William Tyndale and Reginald Pole," *Archiv für Reformationsgeschichte*, 81 (1990): 286-308.

historiography until Sir Geoffrey Elton disposed of it. It also described Thomas Becket's fate after his shrine at Canterbury had been destroyed the previous year. Pole's accomplishments as a writer already stood in inverse proportion to those as a diplomat.

Pole's high standing with the pope led to his appointment in 1541 as legate to Viterbo, one of the two most important provinces of the Papal States. There he collected around him a household that proved to be one of the most important seed beds of the Italian Reformation, if hardly the only. Under Pole's direction, his close friend the poet Marcantonio Flaminio revised the most important text of that Reformation, the *Beneficio di Christo*. A dense amalgam of traditional Benedictine piety, Calvin, Luther, and a liberal admixture of Juan de Valdés, the *Beneficio* allegedly sold as many as 40,000 copies in Venice alone, before it was declared heretical and nearly all copies destroyed. That Pole had already developed many of the *Beneficio*'s ideas in *De unitate* together with his superior position suggest that he should almost be assigned credit for the work, along with Flaminio and its original author, Bendedetto da Mantova. Among others in Pole's orbit was Pietro Carnesecchi, whose investigation by the Inquisition a few years later Pole would help to quash.

Within a year of his appointment to Viterbo, Pole received a much more important assignment when Paul made him one of the three legates to the Council of Trent. Although the council never officially opened in 1542, the occasion gave Pole the chance to meet and begin to develop one of the most important relationships of his life, with Giovanni Morone, in part through the mediation of Vittoria Colonna, the woman Pole adopted as his "second mother" after the execution of the Countess of Salisbury in 1541. Pole's relations to Morone and to Colonna illustrate his genius for intense friendships. The Inquisition's term of art used to describe Morone's fate, "seduction," could be applied with a wider meaning to Pole's impact on his circles. The group of fellow believers around Pole included some of the culturally most significant figures of the *Cinquecento*, among them Michelangelo, who, like Colonna, Pole, and Morone, held views of justification and

Introduction

salvation as entirely dependent on God and took a dim view of most religious institutions. Despite his allegiance to this group, Pole was never very successful in forwarding its interests. His first big chance came in 1541, when at the colloquy of Regensburg his patron Contarini worked out with the German Protestants accords on most contested theological issues. Contarini expected Pole to defend the compromise in the Curia, but Pole left Rome for the summer, leaving that vital task to his life-long friend Alvise Priuli (who had no standing in the case) and the new cardinals Bembo and Federico Fregoso (who had little more). Whatever his reason for shirking his responsibility, it was not that Pole disagreed with Contarini's compromise, as has often been said. It seems much more likely that this is an instance of Pole's predilection for avoiding conflict.

Another even more serious case arose in 1545 when Pole was once again made legate to the council. He allegedly asked the pope for time to write his opinion of what the council should do. *De concilio* (catalogue no. 16), known only in later versions, resulted. The presently available text defends papal primacy more than *De unitate* had by grounding the form of a general council not in Nicaea (where in 325 the Emperor Constantine had taken a hand) but in the council of Jerusalem (ca. 50 C. E., where Pole also had to revise Peter's role relative to Paul). But as in *De unitate*, Pole offered a charismatic interpretation both of the council's matter, everything pertaining to faith, probably deliberately not further defined, and also of its action, which depended completely on "an effusion of the Holy Spirit." Once the council finally began, Pole wrote the opening sermon, which demanded that reform begin with the heads of the church. Pole did not otherwise have much chance to have an effect on the council. Like the emperor, he wished the council to consider reform first and only thereafter doctrine, but the council fathers voted to pursue both simultaneously. One of the very first doctrinal issues debated was justification. Pole once more fled, pleading ill health. In Padua he had to be coerced into giving his opinion of the draft decree. He unrepentantly defended the necessity of justification by faith, leaving little room for good works, but he had not done so at the council, and his position lost. Although he refused to seal or sign the decree, the damage was done.

Still, Pole's standing did not suffer. Paul continued to appoint him to major reform commissions, and when the pope died in 1549, Pole became the leading candidate to succeed him. Some, like Morone, enthusiastically supported him out of fellow-feeling.[5] The largest bloc of cardinals, led by the pope's grandson Alessandro Farnese, probably backed Pole largely because they hoped his "spiritual" agenda, perhaps including dismantling most of the papal financial apparatus, would benefit them. The emperor favored Pole, along with several other candidates, especially a cardinal who was related by marriage to the emperor's client Cosimo I, Duke of Florence. Only the French adamantly refused to have anything to do with Pole.

Less than a week into the conclave, Pole came within one vote of election. He probably lost that vote by refusing to campaign. Although Cardinal Gianpietro Carafa, head since 1542 of the revived Roman Inquisition, attacked Pole as a heretic, his actions did relatively little to undermine Pole's chances. Instead, Pole and Carafa (as the French candidate) deadlocked over and over in a conclave which lasted two months. Pole was not above political maneuvers, and his timing was not always off. Perhaps the most important moment after his near-miss came in the dedication to the sixteen-year-old Cardinal Giulio della Rovere of *De summo pontifice* (catalogue no. 12) on the precise day on which Carafa tried to lure him away from the imperial-Farnese front. The work, which exists in at least three major versions, offered a charismatic view of papal primacy as founded on the blood of the martyrs, not institutional and judicial power. The burden of the published text is that only candidates distinguished by their Christlike humility were suited to election. Had its principles been put into effect, that would have reversed three centuries of papal monarchy. The logjam in the conclave was finally broken by

---

[5] Thomas F. Mayer, "Il fallimento di una candidatura: il partito della riforma, Reginald Pole e il conclave di Giulio III," *Annali dell'Istituto storico italo-germanico in Trento*, 21 (1995): 41-67.

Introduction

a deal between Farnese and the French which led to the election of Julius III (1550-1555). Pole, as the front-runner throughout, acquired tremendous status after Julius's accession. In addition to a large increase in his papal pension on which the otherwise impecunious Pole had to live, Julius honored him with a position, along with several allies, on the congregation of the Inquisition. As he had before, Pole missed the opportunity to forward his agenda for dealing with heresy through gentle means as well as defending his friends when he very quickly ceased to attend meetings.

This decision had immediate ramifications when the Inquisition in 1552 began to investigate several persons close to Pole, principal among them Morone. These investigations enraged Julius, who quashed them, but it could not be missed that Pole had once more stood aside at a crucial moment. Julius, however, was unruffled, and the next year forced Carafa into a reconciliation with Pole, which despite the element of coercion showed every sign of holding, that is, until Pole once again withdrew, this time leaving Rome and heading to Maguzzano on the shores of Lake Garda. Even with the full weight of the pope's authority behind him, Pole preferred to avoid further confrontation.

His departure from Rome proved to have even greater consequences when Mary I unexpectedly acceded to the throne of England in July 1553. As soon as the news reached Rome, Julius appointed Pole legate for the restoration of England, and, in part as a cover, for peace between France and the Empire. Pole now faced the biggest opportunity of his life. He fumbled it. The problem was ecclesiastical property. During the Henrician reformation, the monasteries and many other ecclesiastical establishments had either been dissolved or had their landholdings severely reduced. Those who gained that property, no matter what their religious views, wished to keep it. Pole demanded its return. Mary and the emperor both supported the "possessioners," as they were called, and Charles V aborted Pole's legation by denying permission for him first to pass through imperial territory and then to go to England. For a year Pole refused to budge (see catalogue no. 6). In the interval, the marriage of Mary to Charles's son, the Spaniard Philip, added nationalist prejudice to the other difficulties in the way of restoring the English church. By the time Pole finally returned home and reconciled England in November 1554, almost eighteen months had been lost. Abortive efforts to make peace in early 1554, the time when *Di pace* (catalogue no. 17) was written as an address to the emperor, did not compensate. In fact, Pole's maladroit negotiating left the emperor even more suspicious of him. An international peace conference at Marcq in 1555 led to no more tangible results, beyond underlining the degree to which Pole thought peace-making a spiritual matter.

When Pole finally returned to England, he went to work with a will. Although facing daunting problems, not least of them completely inadequate human resources, both his own and those of the English church, Pole set about repairing the damage done by twenty years of schism. He tried to restore the clergy, traditional worship, monastic life, and above all, the law of the church, but achieved only indifferent results. Two problems proved almost intractable, compounded by constant demands from the queen that Pole provide her with emotional support and take an active role in the government. The first was money. Henry's depredations had left the church in a very serious financial situation, and there was only so much Pole could do quickly about that. This led to the second problem, time. By early 1555 when Pole could get to work, he had only three and a half years left. But on two scores Pole had a major impact, and with more time and money might well have succeeded in restoring the Catholic Church altogether.

His first contribution came on the score of heresy. Unlike Mary and as he had always done, Pole preferred leniency for heretics amounting almost to embryonic toleration.[6] Even in the most high-profile case of Thomas Cranmer, deprived Archbishop

---

[6] Thomas F. Mayer, "'Heretics Be Not in All Things Heretics:' Cardinal Pole and the Potential for Toleration," in J. C. Laursen and C. J. Nederman, eds., *The Roots of Toleration in Europe, 1100-1700: Theory and Practice* (University of Pennsylvania Press, 1997), pp. 107-24.

Introduction

of Canterbury, Pole kept his distance, both literally and figuratively. Although his letters to the imprisoned Cranmer, including the work that would later become *De sacramento* (catalogue no. 7), have been condemned for their savagery, they are not out of line by the notoriously violent standards of sixteenth-century polemic, and *De sacramento* is notable in addition for its continued stress on the importance of faith to salvation. The irony of Pole's handling of Cranmer is how many religious beliefs they shared. Where they divided most sharply was over the issue of authority and obedience. Perhaps already from the time of his cardinalate and certainly by the early 1550s, Pole had come to believe that the individual, no matter how important his conscience (Pole could sound almost like Luther on this score), had to submit to ecclesiastical tradition and to papal authority. Cranmer had done neither. By Pole's lights, Cranmer simply could not point to his "fathers" and therefore must be a heretic. But it was Mary who demanded death. For heretics who were prepared to blame their errors on aberrant ecclesiastical authorities—their bishops, like Cranmer—Pole was prepared to be lenient to the maximum degree, and so instructed his commissioners for heresy. More than that, in every case except Cranmer's and one or two others, Pole gave a second chance to even heinous offenders like the famous preacher Edward Crome or John Cheke. Of the 300 or so Marian executions for religion, only about 10 percent took place under Pole's authority. He might, of course, have done more to prevent them, but under pressure from the queen and from his friend and collaborator Bartolomé Carranza, Pole gave in.

A more unqualified success came in the London synod that Pole called in late 1555. Its canons addressed preaching, clerical discipline, lay piety, and most of the points needing attention, and had they been systematically enforced, would have completely overhauled the English church. Time did not allow. Nevertheless, among its provisions was the establishment of seminaries for the training of the clergy, an idea which passed directly into the legislation of Trent, and through Pole's datary Niccolò Ormanetto to Carlo Borromeo. Pole did what he could to set an example to preachers, writing perhaps as many as twenty sermons and delivering at least some of them (see catalogue no. 10). Though not a great number by comparison with Calvin, for example, given the sensitivity of preaching as an issue in Italy, where it had long been viewed suspiciously, and the massive demands on Pole's time, the number is fairly impressive. Writing undoubtedly contributed to Pole's greatest success, stemming from his patronage of Ellis Heywood (a member of his household in England), Nicholas Harpsfield (his archdeacon of Canterbury), and George Lily (long-time intimate and chaplain as archbishop), through whom he directed the creation of the dominant Catholic view of the early English Reformation.

Pole made progress almost immediately, albeit on nothing like the scale demanded, in no small part thanks to Julius's full backing, and Morone's as protector of England. When Julius died and was succeeded after the brief pontificate of Marcellus II by Carafa as Paul IV, the situation began to look different. For about a year, Rome and England continued to cooperate closely and Pole and Carafa exchanged expressions of high mutual regard. In late 1556, trouble arose between Paul and Philip as King of Naples, and over the next six months the situation steadily worsened. Finally, in May 1557 open war broke out in the vicinity of Rome, and Paul withdrew Pole's legation, which he had previously spared when cancelling all the other legates in Philip's territories. Worse, Paul had Morone arrested in May 1557. War and heresy threatened to undo the groundwork Pole had laid.

Pole, protected by the king and queen, did not back down this time. In a number of missions and several letters, including the forthright "Apology" to Pope Paul (catalogue no. 35), he defended a collective leadership of the church more directly than he had since *De unitate* or the early drafts of "De reformatione" (catalogue no. 8), and underlined his archiepiscopal standing as counterweight to the pope. He made the same point by building a new wing onto Lambeth Palace to house himself and his most important administrators. These could not compensate for the loss of his legation, but Pole continued to try, and by early 1558 could assemble something like a complete accounting of church

Introduction

finances and initiate a plan to transfer surpluses from one diocese to cover shortfalls in another. It had not gotten very far by the time Pole fell mortally ill in September. When he and Mary died in November, within less than a day of each other, their efforts ceased. A phase of both the English and European Reformations had come to an end. Catholic Reform had become Counter-reformation, and Pole had played a central role in the transition.

The Need for a Catalogue

That role was even more significantly played in writing than in action, in which Pole's record was markedly checkered. Strangely, despite steady interest in his works ever since his death, their numerous manuscripts—other than of some of his correspondence—have attracted little serious attention.[7] The most comprehensive catalogue appears in Paul Brassel's canon law thesis, but it can be misleading and has only rarely been cited.[8] The texts of Pole's most famous writing, *De unitate*, have been studied, unfortunately in very unsatisfactory fashion, and cursory reference made to them in one translation.[9] Only one of his books has been critically edited, but without taking account of all the manuscripts, especially not the English versions (see catalogue no. 17).[10] Beyond that, there is only a sketchy codi-

---

[7] For some of the manuscripts of a part of Pole's legatine correspondence in 1553-56, see Lutz, pp. LXXXII-XCV. The present study excludes Pole's letters, for which see *CRP*.

[8] The more extensive version of the catalogue is in "Praeformatio reformationis tridentinae de seminariis clericorum," Pontificia universitas Gregoriana thesis, Rome, 1935, pp. XII-XV and a much shorter excerpt appeared in the published thesis (Roehampton: Manresana, 1938), pp. 11-12. As an example of its unreliability, Brassel identified one version of *De summo pontifice* (BAV, Vat. lat. 5966, fos. 133r-201v) as "Dialogus ad reformationem spectans."

[9] Thomas F. Dunn, "The Development of the Text of Pole's *De unitate ecclesiae*," *Papers of the Bibliographical Society of America*, 70 (1976): 455-68. Noëlle-Marie Egretier, ed., *Défense de l'unité de l'église* (Paris: J. Vrin, 1967), reproduced several pages of the PRO and BAV texts, but did not list the MSS.

[10] Lutz edited Pole's *Oratio di pace* on pp. 381-403. See catalogue no. 17.

cology of one volume.[11] Unsurprisingly, serious scholarship has not made much use of the manuscripts, and the one major exception could have paid more attention to their codicology and palaeography.[12] It is representative that the author of a thesis on Pole's *De summo pontifice* found none of its fourteen manuscripts, comprising at least three independent versions.[13]

Many catalogues of Pole's works have appeared (see the abbreviations above), but they merely repeated the list in the second life of Pole by Andras Dudic with one or two additions of printed works. It was not until the eighteenth century that serious efforts were made to recover Pole's manuscripts. The first important advance came in Hugh Tootell's *The church history of England from the year 1500 to the year 1688, chiefly with regard to Catholicks* (1737), published under the name of Charles Dodd. It is worth noting that the list in the ASV, that in the first life by Ludovico Beccadelli, Dudic's and Tootell/Dodd's are all in part independent of one another, especially Tootell/Dodd's which has ten or twelve items not in Dudic, his principal source for Pole's life. The most important of these new entries were documents at Douai, especially Pole's legatine register.[14] Thomas Tanner pro-

---

[11] Thomas F. Dunn, "Cardinal Reginald Pole and Codex Vaticanus Latinus 5970," *Manuscripta*, 22 (1978): 75-82.

[12] Dermot Fenlon, *Heresy and Obedience in Tridentine Italy: Cardinal Pole and the Counter Reformation* (Cambridge: Cambridge University Press, 1972). Pieces of Pole's correspondence and a few of his writings figure in Massimo Firpo and Dario Marcatto's incomparable work on the *processo* Morone (*PM*).

[13] Martin Trimpe, "Macht aus Gehorsam: Grundmotive der Theologie des päpstlichen Primates im Denken Reginald Poles (1500-1558)," University of Regensburg thesis, 1972.

[14] Tootell's information about Douai apparently did not come from first-hand observation, although he studied there and his hand supposedly appears in the indices to several volumes in the Bibliothèque municipale. Leslie Stephen and Sidney Lee, eds., *Dictionary of National Biography* (Oxford: Oxford University Press, 1917) (hereafter *DNB*), s. n. Dodd, Charles. There is no mention of Pole materials in R. C. Chaplain to an English regiment [Hugh Tootell], *History of the English College at Doway, from its First Foundation in 1568, to the Present Time* (London: printed for Bernard Lintott, 1713), p. 3, which describes the college's two libraries.

Introduction

duced a very thorough bibliography in the early eighteenth century, mainly but not exclusively of printed works, supplemented by Dudic. But as in so many other matters connected to Pole, the real protagonist was Cardinal Angelo Maria Querini. In addition to making reasonably thorough use of the materials in the BAV, some in the ASV, and perhaps the Inquisition's files, he scoured Europe, badgering his contacts for word of Pole's papers.[15] Some of them he managed to acquire, including a copy of the preface to *De unitate* to Edward VI.[16] Other things of which he learned, he ignored, especially Pole's register in Douai, and he apparently missed one vital collection, another late register of Pole's peace and English legations, then still in the Inquisition archives.[17] Despite all his energy, it is not untypical of Querini that his catalogue of Pole's works is a blank page.[18]

A flurry of biographies in the late nineteenth and early twentieth centuries produced no progress beyond Tanner and Querini, and instead one major mistake was perpetrated on the basis of a mistaken reading of Tanner. Walter Farquhar Hook's study, published in 1869, appended a list of Pole's works derived from Tanner, which was then taken over verbatim by Athanasius Zimmermann. The most interesting thing about this list is its third last entry, which makes it appear that a large number of items, including "De modo concionandi," were to be found in the Parker Library of Corpus Christi College, Cambridge.[19] In fact,

---

[15] See BCQ, MS F. III. 7 m. 1, fo. 49r, Thomas Philippe Cardinal d'Alsace-Boussu, probably to Querini, Malines, 7 March 1748, a report on materials in Douai. The text of Pole's preface to Edward VI, published by Querini, probably comes from that in ACDFSO, St. st. E-6-a, but that of his letter to Francisco de Navarra (*CRP*, no. 5733), a copy of which is now found in the same *busta*, does not.

[16] See catalogue no. 2.

[17] Lutz, pp. LXXXVII-XCII. It is all the stranger that Querini did not use this register, since Sforza Pallavicino had leaned heavily on it a century earlier when writing his *Istoria del concilio di Trento*.

[18] BCQ, MS F. III. 7 m. 1, fo. 68r, the conclusion of Querini's autograph brief life of Pole: "Le Opere del Cardinal Polo sono" and then nothing.

[19] Walter Farquhar Hook, *Lives of the Archbishops of Canterbury*, 8 (London:

Tanner's punctuation threw off a careless Hook. Instead of saying that all the works Hook listed were in the Parker Library, Tanner meant only to say that the last, "Statuta academiae Cantabrigiensis," was, as it still is (see catalogue no. 39). No further serious effort to use or find Pole's manuscripts was made until after World War II, when Giuseppe De Luca, a strong admirer of Pole, began a catalogue of his letters and writings. Perhaps knowing that he would never complete the job himself, he tried to interest at least one younger historian in finishing it.[20] In 1954 and then again with John XXIII's permission, De Luca also managed to gain access to the Inquisition's archives.[21] He was permitted to take notes, although he was not allowed to remove them. He probably saw the file of ACDFSO St. st. E- 6-a, but what else may never be known.[22]

There are good reasons for the neglect of Pole's MSS. Locating and cataloguing them presents imposing problems, beginning with their dispersion and the sheer scale of his writing. With understandable exasperation, Benjamin Pye the eighteenth-

---

Richard Bentley, 1869; reprinted 1884), p. 446: "De natali die Christi. Comment. in Esaiam. Comment. in Davidis hymnos. Cathechismum Dialogum de passione Christi [Zimmermann, puzzled by the syntax, inserted a "?" after Cathechismum, where doubtless a period should have gone]. De modo concionandi. Homelias tres. Statuta accademiae Cantabrigiensis, edita 15 Aug. 1557, cap. xv. MS. Coll. Corp. Chr. Cantabr. Miscell." Athanasius Zimmermann, *Kardinal Pole, sein Leben und seine Schriften. Ein Beitrag zur Kirchengeschichte des 16. Jahrhunderts* (Regensburg: F. Pustet, 1893), p. 4.

[20] Conversation with Donald Weinstein, who graciously gave me the note cards listing materials about Pole which De Luca had once given him. They apparently originally came from Cardinal Mercati, sometime librarian of the Vatican Library.

[21] Pagano-Ranieri, pp. 26-7n prints De Luca's request for admission.

[22] Pagano (Pagano-Ranieri, p. 52n). When questioned further in person, Pagano said he does not remember why he thought that, although he had often seen modern lists in blue ink, like those in St. st. E- 6-a, in Inquisition *buste*. (Several requests for a photocopy of one of them for comparison to De Luca's hand were not filled.) For an implicit criticism of Pagano's failure to publish De Luca's notes, see Gigliola Fragnito, "Vittoria Colonna e l'Inquisizione," *Benedictina*, 37 (1990): 157-72, 158-59. The decision was not up to him.

Introduction

century translator of the first life of Pole, summed up Pole's career as author by noting that *De summo pontifice* grew from one book to five, "such was the restless pen of this indefatigable writer!"[23] Despite heavy losses, the surviving works cover about 3,600 folios. And, as the catalogue will make clear, pieces of his archive wound up almost literally strewn across Europe, helping to explain how the losses occurred. The numbering of the individual sections of the largest single piece of his *Nachlass*, the nine volumes in the Biblioteca Apostolica Vaticana, Vaticani latini 5964-72, offers an indication of the original bulk of MSS. The highest number left undeleted is 100, although the highest once written is 109. A total of thirty-three numbered items survive, including two outside the BAV volumes, one in ACDFSO, Stanza storica E-6-a and one in Venice, Biblioteca Marciana, Ms. Lat. IV, 114 (2304), fo. 172r (title page only). The ACDFSO piece almost certainly belongs to the main series. It is a version of the preface to Edward VI for *De unitate*, and its no. 50 places it squarely in the midst of the collection of other such prefaces, including no. 52 which is a fragment of the same work. Not all the rest of these form a single series, and not all of them refer directly to Pole's works. Duplication and changes in numbers indicate that some of the numbering was done at least twice, especially the duplicate 109s deleted on the two texts of *De summo pontifice* subsequently numbered 43 and 44. No. 88 (Vat. lat. 5970, fo. 126r) designates a set of corrections by someone else to the printed text of *De unitate*. Nevertheless, most of the numbers appear to belong together on the grounds of hand.[24] The catalogue below adds another twenty-nine items to the numbered thirty-three, for a total of sixty-two. Assuming that the catalogue entries would once have been part of the series, that means that only between 57 percent and 62 percent (using 109 or 100 as their

---

[23] *The life of Cardinal Reginald Pole, written originally by Lodovico Beccadelli. . .translated by Benjamin Pye* (London: Bathurst, 1766), p. 166n.

[24] The arabic numbers are 3-4, 6, 9-10, 12, 32, 35, 37 (twice, including BNM, 2304), 39-41, 43-45, 46 (twice), 47, 50 (ACDFSO), 52-56 (twice?), 60 (twice), 62, 79, 88, 97, and 100. In addition, Roman numeral IX appears on the work also numbered arabic 12.

total) of Pole's singly enumerated MSS, not necessarily equivalent to individual titles, have survived. If the catalogue entries do not belong to the numbered series, the survival rate is only one-third. One major title may have disappeared without a trace, "De modo concionandi." The disparity between the numbers of works given in the known inventories and another catalogue mentioned in Niccolò Franco's interrogations suggests losses on at least this scale. The longest of the first sort lists only nineteen works, while Franco thought he remembered having seen a catalogue of about fifty titles.[25] Pole's reluctance to divulge his works and eventual secrecy about them make it entirely possible that half or more of them have been lost without leaving any indication that they ever existed.

Another problem is palaeographical and codicological, caused originally by the collective authorship of Pole's works, and exacerbated by later conservators. Pole's stable of authors worked and re-worked his writing, even after some of it had appeared in print. Multiple versions exist of almost every work, and it can be nearly impossible to map the relations between them. Sometimes it appears that a line of development was abandoned and a text begun anew, only to return in the new version to some point in the previous effort. Seven identified hands appear on the manuscripts, as well as an equal number still unknown. The first set includes Pole; Priuli, Venetian noble and Pole's constant companion for more than twenty years; Marcantonio Faita, Pole's principal secretary in the 1550s if not before; Dudic; Gianbattista Binardi, perhaps the most substantial literary figure in Pole's circles after Flaminio, even though he wrote very little; Seth Holland, later Warden of All Souls' College, Oxford; and Henry Pyning, one of Pole's most important men of business, who may have been in his service since the mid-1530s.[26] A grave problem

---

[25] Angelo Mercati, *I costituti di Niccolò Franco (1568-1570) dinanzi l'Inquisizione di Roma esistenti nell'Archivio segreto vaticano* (Vatican City: Biblioteca apostolica vaticana, 1955; Studi e Testi, 178), pp. 180-81.

[26] For all these, see my "When Maecenas was Broke: Cardinal Pole's 'Spiritual' Patronage," *Sixteenth Century Journal*, 27 (1996): 419-35. I intend to return to Pole's household.

Introduction

of conservation compounds the underlying palaeographical difficulties, especially for the manuscripts in the BAV. Large parts of two of them (Vat. lat. 5964 and 5965) and at least some sections of all of them have been virtually destroyed by the pasting of translucent paper or cellophane over many folios. Nearly all of this material has now turned almost completely opaque. Fortunately, these codices were microfilmed about forty years ago, after the "restoration" but before further deterioration, and the microfilms sometimes prove easier to read than the originals.[27] The manner in which the present volumes were assembled also precludes most codicological research.

History of the Manuscripts

One final problem arises from the later history of Pole's manuscripts. Most of the cataloguing was probably Binardi's work, although it is uncertain whether he added the numbers (we shall return to this problem). Binardi had charge of Pole's works in England, and the fact that the catalogue does not include manuscripts left behind suggests that Binardi must have done his work after most of Pole's former household departed.[28] It is difficult to say when, a problem compounded by uncertainty over exactly how Pole's works reached Italy. Although it has usually been thought that Priuli kept them with him, it looks as if at least some of them came with Binardi. Beccadelli hoped in mid-1559 that Priuli would bring Pole's works with him to Italy, and Priuli wrote in December 1559 that he and his companions meant to re-read Pole's works "and have them copied in order to send them into the light for the common utility and in testimony of the

---

[27] They are housed in the Vatican Film Library, St. Louis University. My thanks to Charles Ermatinger and his staff, without whom much of this work could not have been done.

[28] J. I. Tellechea Idigoras, ed., *Fray Bartolomé Carranza. Documentos historicos*, six volumes (Madrid: Real Academia de la Historia, 1962-1981), 2, p. 945, deposition of Francesco Delgado, 15 July 1562.

sincere piety which always reigned in that holy soul."[29] Donato Rullo announced Priuli's intention to Pole's old Tridentine ally Cardinal Girolamo Seripando in mid-1560, writing that Priuli "had the care of the cardinal's said writings as of all other things, and wishes. . .to issue them, and some have already been prepared, but he wished to send them first to Rome and proceed in this according to the order and will of the Cardinal [Morone]." According to a note on the dorse, "scritti di Polo" ("Pole's writings") were enclosed.[30] Carnesecchi maintained during his later investigations by the Inquisition, much of which focused on Pole, that Pole's works had come via Lombardy to Seripando, but not through Morone's hands.[31] Binardi, however, had left for home before Priuli departed from London, and he may already have been at work "reading" Pole's writings in Venice in December 1559. In that case he must have carried them himself, since Priuli did not reach Padua until March 1560.[32] Whoever

---

[29] "[E]t farli copiar per mandar in luce a commune utilità, et in testimonio della sincera pietà che sempre regnò in quel santo animo." BPP, MS. pal. 1010, fos. 298v-99r (*PM*, 5, p. 430n) and BPP, MS pal. 1019/12, 8N.

[30] "[H]ebbe cura delli detti scritti del Cardinale come de tutte l'altre cose, et desidera. . .dare alcuni d'essi fuora, et già si ha preparati alcuni, ma desiderava prima mandarli a Roma et procedere in ciò secondo l'ordine et volere del Cardinale [Morone]." De Frede, p. 123. For Seripando's strongly positive attitude to Pole, see his letter to Tommaso de Villanova of 28 November 1544 (Augustinian Generalate archives, Rome, Reg Dd 21, fos 36v-7v; partially printed in Thomas de Herrera, *Alphabetum Augustinianum* [Madrid, 1643], 2, p. 443 and completely in *Revista Agustiniana*, 1 [1881]: 134f).

[31] *Proc. Carn.*, p. 452.

[32] Binardi left London sometime after 12 August (ASAS, 40/139; Bonelli, no. 161) and reached Modena and then Ferrara by November (ASAS, 40/155; Bonelli, no. 178). For him in Venice, see BAV, Vat. Lat. 6414, fos. 191r-92v, Binardi-Morone, "signore et patrone mio," Venice, 17 December, *s. a.* Fragnito, "Censura," p. 24n says that "con ogni verosimiglianza" the letter belongs to 1561, but I suggest a date of 1559 on the basis of the certainty that Binardi was then in Venice (cf. ASAS, 40/160; Bonelli, no. 183) and on Carnesecchi's letter to Giulia Gonzaga of 25 December 1560 reporting that Binardi was still at work (*Proc. Carn.*, p. 476). Binardi apparently did not go to Rome before early 1561, which may be the time that Pole's MSS finally arrived there. See Faita's letter of 22 March 1560/1 saying that Morone had invited Binardi to Rome (ASAS, 41/67). Binardi may have visited Venice during the last stage of the Council of

Introduction

brought them, Morone still had not received the MSS by September 1560.[33] To complicate matters further, Seripando's involvement may have pre-dated Pole's death. Morone claimed in June 1557 that "I understood that the archbishop [of Salerno, Seripando] saw many of his writings in order to correct them; and he is a learned man who could judge the truth, which I cannot judge, not being learned nor having seen many of his compositions."[34] Seripando had been trying for five years to get various of Pole's works. In May 1555 he had been promised Pole's letter on church property and *De sacramento*.[35] In September he asked again, as well as for the rest of the "tractato della reforma," part of which he had received in Brussels, and Rullo included the canons of the London synod among the works that interested Seripando.[36] Six months later, some should have been sent, but apparently Seripando did not get them.[37] It looks, however, as if Morone may have. "Two little works of Cardinal Pole, one on the sacrament, the other about ecclesiastical goods" were supposed to have been found among the papers sequestered at the time of his arrest.[38]

Trent. Pio Paschini, *Un Amico del Card. Polo: Alvise Priuli* (Rome: Pontificio Seminario Romano Maggiore [*Lateranum*, no. 2], 1921), p. 154 for Priuli's return.

[33] *Proc. Carn.*, p. 448.

[34] "Ho inteso che l'arcivescovo [of Salerno, Seripando] ha veduto molti suoi scritti per corregerli; et è huomo dotto che pot[r]ia giudicare il vero, il che non posso giudicar io, non essendo dotto né havendo veduto molte sue compositioni." *PM*, 2, p. 464. As Firpo and Marcatto note, there is otherwise no information that Seripando was working on Pole's writings before 1560, except for his *votum* on justification for the Council.

[35] De Frede, p. 67.

[36] De Frede, pp. 73 and 104.

[37] De Frede, pp. 100-102.

[38] Bernardo Navagero to Doge and Senato (ASVe, Archivio Proprio Roma, 10, fo. 61v; *CSPV*, 6:2, no. 945 [26 June 1557?]; partially printed in *PM*, 5, "Documenti," no. 35). Navagero wrote that Pole's agent (Antonio Giberti) had told Navagero's secretary that "nelle scritture d'esso reverendissimo Morone sono stato trovate due operine del cardinal Polo, una de sacramento, l'altra de

Cardinal Pole and his Manuscripts

Whenever Seripando undertook his revisions, once he had finished, the MSS on which he had worked were probably sent to Rome. So fairly quickly were some of the rest of Pole's writing. In 1561 Beccadelli, wishing to see the publication of Pole's synodal decrees, thought the MS was to be found together with other writings in Morone's house, and Antonio Giberti, Pole's former agent in Rome, also had a copy.[39] During Carnesecchi's interrogations a few years later the inquisitors asked who had copied Pole's works and where. He thought either Binardi or Faita; if Binardi, the work was done in Venice, if Faita, he did not know.[40] From Franco's testimony not much later, it appears that Faita, who had custody of Pole's works and had copied at least one of them, did so in Rome.[41] The present Vat. lat. 5967 was probably in Faita's charge, to judge from Franco's claim that he had seen a copy of Pole's famous letter to the master of the sacred palace, Girolamo Muzzarelli, in Faita's hand, as is that in 5967 (fos. 358r-65v).[42] Others of Pole's works were to be found in Rome in

---

bonis ecclesiasticis, nelle quali [*PM*: nella quale] tocca i passi importanti de libero arbitrio, de predestinatione, et de purgatorio." Firpo could not identify the works meant, but the first seems likely to have been Pole's second letter to Thomas Cranmer (catalogue no. 7), and the second one (or several) letter(s) or position papers about church property (catalogue no. 6). There is no trace of either in two inventories of Morone's papers in *PM*, 6, pp. 385-414, the first of the books sequestered at the time of his arrest but drawn up in 1559, the other of missing pieces which Morone wanted returned dating from about the same time. Neither the printed text of Pole's letter to Cranmer nor any of the pieces about church property contain discussions of free will, predestination or purgatory.

[39] Fragnito, "Censura," pp. 24n-25.

[40] *Proc. Carn.*, pp. 434-35 and 477-78.

[41] Mercati, *I costituti*, pp. 179-8, 184. Franco also revealed that security had not been perfect. Salustio Viscanti, a corrector for Manuzio's press, had arranged for him to see one of Pole's writings. *I costituti*, pp. 188, 180, 36.

[42] The connection between Faita and BAV, Vat. lat. 5967 is not certain, especially because the inquisitors' description of the letter they showed Franco does not match that in 5967. It was said to be only two folios long and to be found after fo. 80 in a volume several times shown to him. Franco recognized the writing as Faita's, but thought the letter must have been removed from the

Introduction

the 1570s and 1580s, and may have been there earlier. The best evidence comes from the history of *De sacramento* (catalogue no. 7). It was published in Cremona in 1584 by one Deodato Quistri, who said he had gotten the manuscript from his father Philomeno, who had it in turn while in Rome "from Reginald's familiars" ("a familiaribus Reginaldi").

Yet other writings went to Florence in 1566, just as Carnesecchi's trial entered its final phase.[43] Filippo Gheri, one of Morone's longest-term and closest associates, intended them to go either to Carnesecchi or to Beccadelli. Instead, they came to Lelio Torelli, a leading servant of Cosimo de' Medici, who deliberately did not let Gheri know of their arrival in order not to leave a back trail for interested (and evil-intentioned) parties in Rome. What became of them after Torelli returned them to Beccadelli in late summer is unknown, although some of them may have remained with Beccadelli's family until they disappeared or were sold in the eighteenth century.[44] If Gheri's consignment included anything like the fifty titles of his inventory, then this loss would be the single most catastrophic accident to befall Pole's papers.

Perhaps the most important episode in the history of Pole's MSS came in the competition to publish his works that arose even before his death. The first race to the press was over *De unitate*, which Cardinal Carafa, joined by Pole's strong ally Muzzarelli, had urged him to release in 1553.[45] Muzzarelli suggested that other writings be issued as well. Pole replied that the decision

---

volume in which he had originally seen it, given that it was now in a different codex. Then again, the likely content of the letter would square with that in 5967, since the inquisitors were concerned to trace an *apologia* Pole had written against Paul IV. Mercati, *I costituti*, p. 181.

[43] Fragnito, "Censura," pp. 17-20.

[44] See the inventory of the contents of the Beccadelli archive in Bologna sent by Senator Ludovico Beccadelli in response to Benedict XIV's request in BAV, Vat. Lat. 12909, fos. 26r-28r. The covering letter is dated 21 December 1743. The largest part of this corpus was composed of correspondence, most of which is now lost.

[45] Muzzarelli's letter is lost, but its content can be reconstructed from Pole's reply of 9 August 1553 (*CRP*, no. 636, including its complicated textual history).

was up to the pope.[46] Pole insisted that he was not a writer, and that publication was the equivalent of preaching, for which he had no license. Julius III had agreed, to the extent of urging Pole not to publish the defense Carafa had asked him to write, and assuring Pole that he would protect his reputation. Nevertheless, Pole was still willing to publish, if the pope so ordered. Muzzarelli did not relax his pressure, replying that he had always thought Pole should publish his work.[47] Mary's accession superseded the debate, and Pole said nothing further. Nevertheless, it looks as if Julius did not let the matter drop. The manuscript of Pole's "De summo pontifice" in the Inquisition's archives bears a permission to publish granted by Pier Paolo Giannerini, Master of the Sacred Palace (the official papal theologian), conditional on the Vicar of Rome's approval.[48] It can be dated with fair confidence to about the time of the exchange between Pole and Muzzarelli. Giannerini succeeded Muzzarelli in December 1553 as Master of the Sacred Palace, and died in 1557.[49] It seems very likely that Giannerini's

---

[46] In the version in BAV, Vat. lat. 5967 he merely left it to Muzzarelli.

[47] *CRP*, no. 670.

[48] ACDFSO, St. st. E-6-a, fasc. 5, fo. 76v, note at foot: "Imprimatur sed a S. D. N. R.mo Vic. prius videretur: Frater Petrus Paulus Giannarinus de Arrectio Magister Sacri Palatii [new line] Vir. (?)." This was the standard form of an imprimatur for a work to be published in Rome as established by the Fifth Lateran Council in 1515. Mansi, 32, c. 913.

[49] Heinrich Lutz, ed., *Nuntiaturberichte aus Deutschland 1533-1559 nebst ergänzenden Aktenstücke*, 14, *Nuntiatur des Girolamo Muzzarelli Sendung des Antonio Agustín Legation des Scipione Rebiba* (Tübingen: Niemeyer, 1971), p. XIX. The most reliable source for the date of Giannerini's death is Pio Tommaso Masetti, *Monumenta et antiquitates veteris disciplinae ordinis praedicatorum* (Rome: Ex typographia reverendae camerae apostolicae, 1864), 2, pp. 50-53, which cites both the necrology of the convent of Bibbiena, where Giannerini was professed in 1512, and a commemorative medal in the Biblioteca Casanatense. Masetti gave the precise date of 29 June, but on uncertain evidence. Innocenzo Taurisano, "Fra Girolamo Savonarola (Da Alessandro VI a Paolo IV)," *La Bibliofilia*, 55 (1953), pp. 14-53, p. 24n followed Masetti (cf. *PM*, 4, p. 195n), but in *Hierarchia ordinis praedicatorum, pars prima* (Rome: Manuzio, 1916), p. 53 Taurisano had 1558, which is the date adopted by most commentators. Cf. Angelo Maria Walz, *I domenicani al concilio di Trento* (Rome: Herder, 1961), p. 183; Paolo Simoncelli, "Momenti e figure del savonarolismo romano," *Critica*

Introduction

imprimatur came earlier rather than later in his tenure, because by its end he was very much in Paul IV's disfavor. He had been violently chased out of a consistory in May 1557 when he had

---

Storica, 11 (1974), pp. 47-82, p. 60n; *PM*, 6, pp. 180-81n. The confusion about the date probably arises from Giannerini's involvement in Savonarola's troubles, which reached the stage of formal proceedings only in 1558. Massimo Firpo and Paolo Simoncelli, "I processi inquisitoriali contro Savonarola (1558) e Carnesecchi (1566-1567): una proposta di interpretazione," *Rivista di storia e letteratura religiosa*, 18 (1982), pp. 200-252. They had, however, begun in 1556, the date given by Tommaso Neri in his account of how he undertook Savonarola's defense. That was when one of the pope's familiars leaked word to the Dominican general Stefano Usodimare, who intrusted the reply to Neri. Tommaso Neri, *Apologia del reverendo Fra Tommaso Neri fiorentino dell'ordine de' frati Predicatori in difesa della dottrina del R. P. F. Girolamo da Ferrara del medesimo ordine* (Florence: Giunti, 1564), dedication, sig. A4r-v. Usodimare died in March 1557 (Taurisano, *Hier. ord. praed.*, p. 11). Neri shortly thereafter left Rome, which may explain why he made no mention of Giannerini. The date of Neri's initial involvement is confirmed by an anonymous report of February 1557 that "Thomas Nerius. . .scripsit Apologiam" (BAV, Vat. lat. 4663, fos. 163v-64r, fo. 163v; cf. Simoncelli, "Savonarolismo romano," pp. 53-4n, who raises difficulties about the date, but does not cite Neri's own testimony). But according to the earliest source, Vincenzo Ercolani's letter of 1559, Giannerini was the first to defend Savonarola publicly before the pope and cardinals, and immediately found himself confronted by Cardinal Scotti. He died shortly thereafter. Ercolani, "Lettera. . .quando era priore nella Minerva di Roma, scritta ai suoi frati di S. Marco di Firenze, dove si racconta l'esamina fatta sopra la dottrina di Girolamo Savonarola et altre cose accadute a ciò." John Rylands University Library, Manchester, MS Ital. 10, fos. 8v-9v, printed in Bartolommeo Aquarone, *Vita di fra Jeronimo Savonarola*, two volumes, (Alessandria: Carlo Astuti, 1857-58), 2, doc. I, p. XXIX. Cf. Simoncelli, "Savonarolismo romano," p. 60 and Benedetto Carderi, "Messe all'Indice le opere del Savonarola?," *Memorie domenicane*, n. s. 36 (1960): 37-52, pp. 42-43. Thus Carderi would seem to have the chronology right. See also Michele Scaduto, "Lainez e l'indice del 1559: Lullo, Sabunde, Savonarola, Erasmo," *Archivum historicum societatis Jesu*, 24 (1955): 3-32, pp. 6-8 for the beginning of the commission for the Index's interest in 1556. Jacques Quétif and Jacques Echard, *Scriptores ordinis praedicatorum* (Paris: Ballard and Simart, 1721), pp. 166-67 put Giannerini's death in 1564. There is also a mysterious entry in the Papal Master of Ceremony's diary noting the death of an unnamed Master of the Sacred Palace on 27 August 1559 (*CT*, 2, p. 518). It may be worth noting that Neri, Giannerini, and Ercolani all could have had ties to Pole. *PM*, 6, p. 217 (Neri); 4, p. 195 and 6, pp. 180-81 and 295 (Giannerini); Simoncelli, "Savonarolismo romano," p. 52 (Ercolani's teaching in Viterbo).

opposed the pope's wishes over a dispensation for the Constable Montmorency's son's remarriage, publicly defended Savonarola, and dressed down Paul's chief collaborator, Bernardino Scotti, the cardinal of Trani, for leading the charge against his Dominican confrère.[50] Paul had also begun again to proceed against Pole and his circles in 1556.[51] Whatever the date, there remains a question about how Giannerini's *imprimatur* got on the work, since Pole left Rome for Maguzzano in May 1553.[52] There can be no doubt of the work's provenance, since it is almost certainly in Faita's hand, or if not, Dudic's, and he probably joined Pole's household about the time Pole left Rome.[53] Did Pole perhaps accede to Muzzarelli's blandishments and send the work back? Was it inadvertently left behind? If either, how did the work find its way back to Pole, as it almost certainly did?

Pole himself planned to publish *De summo pontifice*, which he spent his enforced leisure in Brussels in 1554 polishing. There is no documentary evidence to link his decision to Giannerini's and Muzzarelli's actions, but the coincidence in time looks suspicious, and the manuscript evidence may mean that Pole sought Giannerini's *imprimatur*. Even more interesting, he, Priuli and Beccadelli provided a subvention to Paolo Manuzio's press at just the time of the correspondence with Muzzarelli, perhaps in

---

[50] For the dispensation, see Navagero to Doge and Senato (ASVe, Archivio Proprio Roma, 9, fo. 167r; *CSPV*, 6:2, no. 879, 8 May 1557). For Savonarola's *processo*, see the last note.

[51] Dario Marcatto, *Il processo inquisitoriale di Lorenzo Davidico (1555-1560). Edizione critica* (Florence: Leo S. Olschki, 1992) and Massimo Firpo, *Nel labirinto del mondo. Lorenzo Davidico tra santi, eretici, inquisitori* (Florence: Leo S. Olschki, 1992) for Lorenzo Davidico's investigation, which revealed many damaging things about Priuli.

[52] *CRP*, no. 610.

[53] The date is an inference from Manuzio's recommendation of Dudic to Priuli in September 1553. *Lettere volgari di M. Paolo Manutio, divise in quattro libri* (Venice: Aldus, 1560), sig. 42v-43r; cf. Ester Pastorello, *L'epistolario manuziano. Inventario cronologico-analitico 1483-1597* (Florence: Leo S. Olschki, 1957), no. 514.

Introduction

preparation for a publication of the work.[54] That Pole meant to issue it not too much later emerges from his request to the Louvain theologians Ruard Tapper and Josse Ravesteyn (Jodochus Tiletanus or Diletanus) for corrections of the work, or perhaps Tapper asked for the opportunity.[55] Those suggestions would have amounted to another species of *imprimatur*, given Tapper's standing as dean of the faculty of theology. Pole promised Tapper to return the work for printing as soon as he had gone over it one more time. It seems likely that Tapper intended to use his printer, Martin Verhasselt.[56] By the time of their correspondence, however, Pole had gone to London and the plan was never executed.[57]

Pole regretted that he could not send Tapper other pieces for publication, because he had promised them to Cardinal Otto Truchsess. Truchsess had joined those trying to convince Pole to publish *De unitate*. Among the other works to which Pole referred was its preface addressed to Edward VI, in which Truchsess had displayed strong interest. Pole gave him permission to publish, but no edition is known (see catalogue no. 2). Instead, Truchsess had to watch Pier Paolo Vergerio precede him into print in either late 1554 or early 1555 (for the edition and the date, see catalogue no. 1). Nothing else appeared under Truchsess's auspices before Pole's death, but almost immediately thereafter his printer in Dillingen, Sebald Mayer, issued Pole's *Testamentum vere christianum* (catalogue no. 18), which became one of the principal instruments in a somewhat misguided effort to portray Pole as a

---

[54] Ibid.; cf. nos. 513, 515; for Beccadelli see Fragnito, "Censura," p. 27.

[55] *CRP*, no. 1029. For Tapper (1487-1559), see especially H. de Jongh, *L'ancienne faculté de théologie de Louvain au premier siècle de son existence (1532-1540)* (Louvain: HES, 1980; reprint of Louvain 1911 ed.), pp. 180-86.

[56] Henri de Vocht, "Ruard Tapper," *Biographie nationale de Belgique* (Brussels: Bruylant, 1924-26), 24, cc. 555-77, c. 565. For Verhasselt, see Anne Rouzet, *Dictionnaire des imprimeurs, librairies et éditeurs des XVe et XVIe dan les limites géographiques de la belgique actuelle* (Nieuwkoop: B. De Graaf, 1975), p. 234.

[57] *CRP*, no. 1029.

loyal son of the Holy See.[58]

From that moment, the efforts to publish Pole's writings intensified. Perhaps without knowing of Mayer's priority, Morone, Seripando and others took up Priuli's proposal, in part as a way to defend themselves from Paul IV by burnishing Pole's memory.[59] It is an interesting irony that the only surviving manuscript of a Pole composition which probably came from Seripando—of *De concilio*—is not the version which appeared in print.[60] Nevertheless, that work was Morone's and Seripando's first effort. One of the principal movers of the project was Egidio Foscarari, a former Master of the Sacred Palace, who had been imprisoned at the same time as Morone. Foscarari explicitly wished the work to serve as a polemic in Pole's defense, and also as a vademecum for all the delegates assembled at Trent. Foscarari further recommended that the legates officially approve the work in order to prevent scholastic theologians from attacking it for its "sweetest style of writing, different from that thorny one the schools use."[61] He suggested that Seripando do the revision, and his plan was accepted.[62] Binardi, Faita, and apparently Alvise Contarini served as copyists and in Binardi's case, at least, correctors. Alvise was the nephew of Pole's first and most important Roman patron. Pole tracked his progress through

---

[58] My thanks to my former student John Frymire for checking the catalogue of Mayer editions. *Proc. Carn.*, pp. 294ff. for negative reactions to Pole's will.

[59] For the fullest treatment, see Fragnito, "Censura," passim and Gigliola Fragnito, *Memoria individuale e costruzione biografica* (Urbino: Argalìa, 1978; Pubblicazioni dell'Università di Urbino, 39) especially p. 17 for Morone's prominence.

[60] BNN, MS VII C. 46. There are many small grammatical variations, but the biggest difference is that the marginal headings in the MS are not picked up in print, nor is there any sign on the MS that it was used for Manuzio's edition. For example, it lacks casting-off marks.

[61] *CT*, 8, pp. 247-8.

[62] *Proc. Carn.*, pp. 435-37, 443, 447-48, 484-87. Seripando worked on the rest of Pole's writings for several years, but was unable to complete the job, Carnesecchi thought because he was too busy.

Introduction

another nephew, Placido, in 1553.[63] Contarini, a student of Pole's old tutor Lazzaro Bonamico and of Manuzio, did not begin his official career as historiographer of Venice until December 1562, so his copying must have come before that. He was later largely responsible for the publication of the 1571 Paris edition of Contarini's works.[64]

Manuzio undertook the publication of *De concilio*, coordinating his efforts with Seripando.[65] This was Cardinal Ercole Gonzaga's suggestion. He perhaps independently also proposed publication of Pole's works, and suggested that Seripando, Foscarari, Beccadelli, Thomas Goldwell, another long-time familiar of Pole, or Dudic prepare *De concilio*.[66] Gonzaga, regent of Mantua and a principal imperialist, had been a supporter of Pole from the early 1540s. It was also his idea, like Foscarari, to have *De concilio* distributed to the council of Trent, two hundred copies being sent for that purpose.[67] Although Manuzio's edition thus enjoyed great success, the campaign did not get very far beyond it. This time it was at least coordinated with Mayer, whose text of *De concilio*, also of 1562, is virtually identical to Manuzio's.[68] Aside from that book, only *Reformatio Angliae* (the

---

[63] *CRP*, no. 686.

[64] Emmanuele Antonio Cicogna, *Delle inscrizioni veneziane*, eight volumes (Venice: Giuseppe Orlandelli, 1824-1853), 2, pp. 244-46; Fragnito, "Censura," pp. 42ff; and *DBI*, 28, pp. 78-82.

[65] Pastorello, *L'epistolario manuziano*, nos. 1037 and 1040.

[66] Filippo Gheri-Morone, Trent, 21 December 1561 (BAV, Vat. lat. 6409, fo. 271r). Henry Damien Wojtyska, *Cardinal Hosius, Legate to the Council of Trent* (Rome: Pontificia Universitas Gregoriana, 1967; Studia ecclesiastica, 3), p. 73 incorrectly asserted that Hosius wrote the preface.

[67] Josef Šusta, *Die Römische Kurie und das Konzil von Trient unter Pius IV. Actenstücke zur Geschichte der Konzil von Trient im Auftrage des Historischen Commission der Kaiserliche Akademie der Wissenschaften*, four volumes (Vienna: A. Hölder, 1904-14), 1, p. 76 and ASV, Conc. Trid. 42, fos. 177r-78v and 205r-6v.

[68] See also Curt F. Bühler, "Observations on the 1562 Editions of Cardinal Reginald Pole's *De Concilio* and *Reformatio Angliae*," *Studies in Bibliography*, 26 (1973): 232-34.

decrees of Pole's legatine synod of 1555-56) and the possibly spurious *De baptismo Constantini* appeared, both also from Manuzio's and Mayer's presses.

The first two biographies of Pole, by Beccadelli and Dudic, entered into this effort to publish his works, as well as providing evidence that his MSS must once have been at the council of Trent, where the two wrote their lives. Both works manifest strong verbal parallels to some of Pole's texts.[69] Beccadelli's biography, finished in December 1561, might have served as an introduction to a Pole edition.[70] Both included inventories of his writings, especially Dudic's highly descriptive one, and expressed the wish that they would soon be printed. Their lists are not identical, any more than are their biographies.[71] They gave in common *De unitate*; *De concilio*, although Dudic did not identify it as printed; *De summo pontifice* (*intra conclavi*), of which only Dudic noted the *extra conclavi* continuation; "De modo concionandi"; and commentaries on the Psalms. After that, their tallies diverged. Beccadelli listed only one more work, *Reformatio Angliae*, which Dudic did not include. Instead, he cited "Libellus de Ecclesia ad veterem morum ac disciplinae formam, revocanda," which is probably "De reformatione ecclesiae," plus "Libellus de restituendis Ecclesiae bonis, ad Philippum, & Mariam, Angliae Reges;" "Libellus item de natali die Christi, Servatoris nostri;" *Oratio de pace*; "Commentarios in Esaiam;" "Catechismus;" and "de Passione Christi Dialogus."[72] It is of great interest that Dudic

---

[69] As one example, compare Pole's wording in his letter to Bartolomé Carranza of 20 June 1558, found only in BAV, Vat. lat. 5967 (*CRP*, no. 2252), with Dudic's summary of Pole's attitude to preaching. Pole wrote "Cum enim in ipsa metropolitana ecclesia et nonnullis illis dioecesis meae locis praedicavi saepius, tum etiam Londini bis, neque posthac, juvante Dei gratia, ut spero, deerit," and Dudic gave "alias quoque concionatus est, & maxime Cantuariae in Ecclesia sua, ac nonnullis in locis, quae sua Dioecesi continebantur." Andras Dudic, *Vita Reginaldi Poli*, in *ERP*, 1, p. 40.

[70] Fragnito, "Censura," p. 23 and *Memoria individuale*, p. 17.

[71] See the introduction to my forthcoming edition and translation of Beccadelli's and Dudic's lives.

[72] Beccadelli, pp. 331-32; Dudic, pp. 62-63.

could expand Beccadelli's catalogue by taking advantage of his time in Pole's household in 1555-56 when he probably worked on Pole's most incendiary books. It is also curious that Dudic gave physical descriptions of some of the volumes. Since his was the life that was published (in 1563), it, in particular, and this campaign in general may well have been among the remote causes of the Roman Inquisition's renewed interest in Pole's unpublished writings.[73] Dudic's collaborator Binardi died in 1566, which absolves him and his catalogue from direct complicity with the inquisitors.[74]

The attempted rehabilitation of Pole under Pius IV stopped abruptly when Pius V replaced him in the year of Binardi's death. Carnesecchi's final interrogations before his execution in 1567 provided the proximate cause of the Inquisition's attention. The inquisitors not only wanted to know all about the publication of Pole's works, but also where to find the rest of them. Carnesecchi pointed them to Priuli's heirs, who must therefore have recovered them from Trent.[75] That lead proved accurate. The works turned up in the hands of Matteo Priuli, Alvise's nephew and sometime familiar of Pole, and Faita had copied most of them. Armed with this information, the inquisitors picked up the trail. Cardinal Scipione Rebiba ordered Priuli in early 1568 to turn over his collection to the nuncio in Venice.[76] The nuncio received no word about what to do with it, and therefore wrote Cardinal Bonelli (the cardinal nephew and Chamberlain) for instructions. Bonelli ordered an inventory sent to Rome by the most secure route on 20

---

[73] Why Dudic should have tried to "unmask" Pole, if he did, is unknown. Even after he went over to the Reformation a few years later, he preserved his respect for his erstwhile patron. Thomas F. Mayer, "A Sticking-plaster Saint? Autobiography and Hagiography in the Making of Reginald Pole," in Mayer and D. R. Woolf, eds., *The Rhetorics of Life-Writing in Early Modern Europe* (Ann Arbor: University of Michigan Press, 1995), pp. 205-22, pp. 210-11.

[74] Cf. the numerous documents about the disputed election after Binardi's death in Archivio di stato, Padua, Corporazioni Soppresse, Capitolo di Piove di Sacco, including b. 33, no. 48, dated 6 October 1566.

[75] *Proc. Carn.*, pp. 477-78.

[76] Pagano-Ranieri, p. 49.

March, and it was duly dispatched on the 23rd. Everything the nuncio had was sent to Rome on 25 August.[77] This may have been highly unfortunate, since it is possible that most of it is now lost, whether at the hands of the popular rioters who sacked the Inquisition archives in Tor di Ripetta at Paul IV's death, or the French who transported a very large part of the remainder to Paris in 1810, where much of it was sold as scrap paper or otherwise destroyed, or the Roman republicans of the mid-nineteenth century who sometimes helped themselves to Inquisition documents.[78] In any case, almost nothing is left in the ACDFSO.

It is possible that the inventory is ASV, Misc. Arm. II 79, fo. 363r. The strongest evidence is the appearance in one of its entries of language virtually identical to that used in ACDFSO, St. st. E-6-a. Misc. Arm. II 79 describes "De reformatione ecclesiae" as a work "in which among others is considered the manner in which holy scripture must be studied, and of the observations of holy days commanded by holy mother church" ("nel quale inter alia si tratta del modo che si deve tenere ne studiar le scrittura sacra, et delle osservatione delle feste commandate dalla S. Madre Chiesa"), and at the foot of St. st. E-6-a, fasc. 4, fo. 23r is a note which apparently says "[t]hese two heads of the holy scriptures and ceremonies must be considered more carefully" ("[q]uesti dui capi de le sacris scripturis et de le ceremoniis accurantia (?) sunt considerandum"), referring to "De summo pontifice." The provenance of Misc. Arm. II 79 in the Gualteruzzi chancellery may reduce the likelihood that it is the Inquisition's list at the same time as it probably means that the Gualteruzzi, among the closest allies of Pole's alignment, also took an interest in his works.[79] It may also be that Misc. Arm. II

---

[77] Pagano-Ranieri, p. 50.

[78] John A. Tedeschi, "The Dispersed Archives of the Roman Inquisition," in *The Prosecution of Heresy: Collected Studies on the Inquisition in Early Modern Italy* (Binghamton, NY: MRTS, 1991; Medieval and Renaissance Texts and Studies, 78), pp. 23-45 and Sergio M. Pagano, ed., with Antonio G. Luciani, *I documenti del processo di Galileo Galilei* (Vatican City: Archivio vaticano, 1984; Collectanea archivii vaticani, 21), pp. 19-22 and 38.

[79] For the Gualteruzzi family of professional secretaries, see Ornella Moroni,

Introduction

79 is earlier. It is entitled "Note of the works which were found at Cardinal Pole's death among his compositions and writings" ("Nota delle opere che si sono trovate alla morte del Car. Polo tra le sue compositioni et scritture") and it refers to "the synod recently held in the kingdom of England" ("la sinodo fatta ultimamente nel regno d'Anglia"), that is, in 1555-56. On the other hand, it is certainly an index of Vat. lat. 5964-72, although not a comprehensive one. Probably only the entry for the elusive "De modo concionandi" may not refer to that collection, and it also does not cite anything now found in Vat. lat. 5970-71, and perhaps not in 5966.

What of Pole's other works in Rome? Who could those *familiares Reginaldi* who gave Quistri *De sacramento* have been? Binardi and Faita (along with Giberti) were there, although I have found no evidence to support a particularly vicious canard about Binardi's activities.[80] Aside from these two, much of Pole's central administration came to Rome, but it is not known whether they carried any of his papers. The tide began in 1555-56 with Antonio Fiordibello and Mariano Vittori, and was swelled in the 1560s by Vincenzo Parpaglia, Ormanetto, and Goldwell. The first three probably left Pole too early to have taken away any works. Fiordibello became an important cog in the papal bureaucracy, and Vittori entered Morone's service.[81] Parpaglia, once Pole's

---

Carlo Gualteruzzi (1550-1577) e i corrispondenti (Vatican City: Biblioteca apostolica vaticana, 1984; Studi e testi, 307), which must be used with great care.

[80] Ludovico Castelvetro claimed that Binardi became a visitor of the Roman prisons. "Vita di Bignardi," Biblioteca Estense, Modena, MS. Alpha H. 1. 11, no. 16, fo. 445r-v (printed by both Girolamo Tiraboschi, *Biblioteca modenese o notizie della vita e delle opere degli scrittori nati degli stati del serenissimo signor duca di Modena*, four volumes [Modena: Società tipografica, 1781], 1, p. 275 and Giuseppe Cavazzuti, *Ludovico Castelvetro* [Modena: Società tipografica modenese, 1903], appendix, pp. 7-8). There is no such general title in G. B. Scanaroli, *De visitatione carceratorum libri tres* (Rome: Reverenda Camera Apostolica, 1675), p. 78, nor does Binardi appear in any of Scanaroli's lists of visitors of individual prisons. Most of Castelvetro's information cannot be confirmed, but what has been proves correct.

[81] Fiordibello went to Rome on Pole's behalf in February 1555, and asked the

most important diplomatic agent, later served as ambassador of the duke of Savoy for much of the 1560s and 1570s, after leaving Pole as Vittori had in 1556.[82] Ormanetto served in the new office of *riformatore* of the diocese of Rome beginning in 1566, and earlier had charge of many of Pole's most important records.[83] Goldwell came to Rome more or less permanently in about 1565.[84] Finally, the relatively unimportant Michele Facchetto, who like many of Pole's former dependents joined Morone's service and seems to have been both a secretary and a bodyguard (a not uncommon combination), also left England too early to interest us.[85] Pyning wanted to go to Rome after travelling to Italy with Priuli, but did neither.[86]

Whatever papers came to Rome, when, and by what agency,

---

pope for permission to stay. ASV, A. A. I-XVIII, 5358 (*CRP*, no. 1079) and 6542. For his career as a papal secretary see René Ancel, "La secretairerie pontificale sous Paul IV," *Revue des questions historiques*, 79 (1906): 408-70, esp. pp. 451-62. Vittori, likewise on a mission from Pole, arrived in Rome in mid-1556, between 9 and 13 June (*CRP*, nos. 1582 and 1615). For his later life see Angelo Sacchetti Sassetti, *La vita e gli scritti di M. Vittori* (Rieti: Trinchi, 1917), pp. 38ff.

[82] *CRP*, no. 1558. For Parpaglia in early 1560 see, e.g., ASAS, 41/164.1 (Bonelli, no. 188; printed in *PM*, 5, pp. 587-8).

[83] Alberto Monticone, "L 'applicazione del concilio di Trento a Roma. I 'Riformatori' e l'Oratorio (1566-1572)," *Rivista di storia della chiesa in Italia*, 8 (1954): 21-48.

[84] *DNB*, s. n., p. 99 to be replaced by my article in *New DNB*. He spent several months in Rome in 1561. T. E. Bridgett and T. F. Knox, *The True Story of the Catholic Hierarchy Deposed by Queen Elizabeth* (London: Burns and Oates, 1889), p. 234.

[85] Franco's claim that he was a member of Pole's household in England is unsubstantiated (Mercati, *I costituti*, p. 179). He may perhaps have been the Michele whom Binardi greeted in various letters along with other of Pole's servants. See, e.g., ASAS, 40/160 (Bonelli, no. 183). He was in Rome through the early 1560s, writing thence about one hundred letters to Pole's former auditor Gianfrancesco Stella. See, e.g., *PM*, 5, pp. 587-8 and Bonelli for the inventory of letters. Faita noted in a letter of March 1560/1 that Facchetto could not write that day "per essere di guardia."

[86] ASAS, 40/135 (Bonelli, no. 157).

Introduction

there had already been losses, or at least misplacements. Probably all of the losses calculated above except for "De modo concionandi" came early on, to judge from the fact that all the entries in Dudic's catalogue, again except "De modo concionandi," are still extant (it may be that this work also still exists, hidden under the guise of some other writing). Priuli, who had a reputation for incompetence in practical affairs, seems not to have been much better at preserving Pole's papers. Quite a few of them were left behind in England, most importantly his "Apology" to Paul IV. The Spanish ambassador, the conde de Feria, knew this piece's importance, and asked Queen Elizabeth to send it to him, as she had other of Pole's writings, apparently from a trunk of them in Elizabeth's possession, but he never received it.[87] Whatever these other papers were, they too have apparently vanished. A good part of Feria's master King Philip's papers from England went down in a shipwreck in 1559, and Feria's own archive has also disappeared.[88] The "Apology" was not all that then remained in England, most of the rest of which came to John Foxe and thence via John Strype to the British Library and the Inner Temple Library, after further losses.[89] Matthew Parker,

---

[87] *Doc. Hist.*, 2, p. 897 and J. I. Tellechea Idigoras, Fray *Bartolomé Carranza y el Cardenal Pole. Un navarro en la restauración católica (1554-1558)* (Pamplona: CIES, 1977) p. 278, Feria to Philip II, London, 29 April 1558: "La Apologia del Cardenal asta ora no a polido aver; ha me dicho la Reyna que hara ver si esta en una arca de papeles del Cardenal que ella tiene y se se alla, me la dara." Philip asked about the "Apology" in March 1559, in April Feria reported that Elizabeth had promised to have a search made for it in a trunk of Pole's papers, and in May Philip was still urging him to get and bring it back himself or give it to Alvaro de la Quadra. M. A. S. Hume, ed., *Calendar of Letters and State Papers Relating to English Affairs Preserved Principally in the Archives of Simancas*, 4 volumes (London: HMSO, 1892-1899), 1, nos 20, 29-30. Four years later, Rullo asked Sir John Legh to have a copy made for which he would be glad to pay. Joseph Stevenson, ed., *Calendar of State Papers, Foreign Series, of the Reign of Elizabeth, 1563* (London: Longman, Green & Co., 1869), no. 73.

[88] "The Count of Feria's Dispatch to Philip II of 14 November 1558," ed. M. J. Rodríguez Salgado and Simon Adams, *Camden Miscellany*, 28 (Camden fourth ser., no. 29; London: Royal Historical Society, 1984), p. 303.

[89] Among the volumes once in Foxe's possession are BL, Harley 417 and Lansdowne 388 and Inner Temple Library, Petyt MS 538/46, fos. 391r-426v, Pole's "Apologia" to Paul IV.

Cardinal Pole and his Manuscripts

Pole's immediate successor at Canterbury, may also have made an effort to collect material connected to Pole, but aside from a version of his synodal decrees and one letter, nothing else is now found in the Parker Library.[90] Other papers, including a manuscript of at least one authentic work, *De summo pontifice*, but above all Pole's final legatine register, stayed in Flanders with Pyning.[91] One or two pieces of Pole's archive may as an outside possibility have remained in Venice, perhaps in the hands of Contarini's heirs. They include the Biblioteca Marciana MS of *De unitate* and perhaps a letter. Both came from Girolamo Contarini's bequest in 1843.[92]

The largest single piece of Pole's corpus, BAV, Vat. lat. 5964-72, probably comprising the materials brought back by

---

[90] MS 121, no. 11 and MS 106, no. 332. My thanks to Mrs. G. Cannell, deputy librarian of the Parker Library, for much assistance. Parker may also have owned *Oratio di pace*. His son John included it among the books he left to his own son (LPL, MS 737, fo. 153r). Two other of Pole's successors as archbishop, John Whitgift and Richard Bancroft, owned copies of his works, Bancroft *De summo pontifice* (LPL H1805.P6), and both he and Whitgift *De concilio* (H820.P6 t. 1 and G720), as well as *De unitate* (H5067.A5). The last was also supposed to be available at Court, where a reading of it may have converted the poet William Alabaster. Henry Foley, *Records of the English Province of the Society of Jesus*, seven volumes (London: Burns and Oates, 1877-1883), 1, p. 67. Whitgift, at least, may have used Pole's books to keep track of his subversive progeny. He surely did not have a high opinion of Pole, whom he lumped with the dangerous Nicholas Sander in a letter to Burghley of 1594. Historical manuscripts commission, *Report on the manuscripts of the Marquess of Salisbury*, 9:5 (London: HMSO, 1894), p. 141.

[91] Cf. the title page of *Treatie of Iustification* (Louvain: Fowler, 1569), which claimed that it had been found among Pole's writings left in the hands of "Henrie Pyning, Chamberlaine and General Receiver to the said Cardinal, late deceased in Louvaine." It is also possible that the register went to Rome and thence to the English College, Douai through the agency of Cardinal William Allen, who wanted at one point copies of "omnia illa quae ad Car.lis Poli legationem pertinent." ASV, Misc. Arm. II 84, fo. 139r-v, without date, although it must be after Allen was made cardinal in 1587; printed in P. Renold, ed., *Letters of William Allen and Richard Barrett 1572-1598* (London: Catholic Record Society, 58, 1967), pp. 194-5.

[92] Dunn, "*De unitate*," p. 456. The manuscript is BNM, Ms. Lat. IV, 114 (2304), fos. 1r-171v and the original letter of 1532 is MS Ital. VII, Cod. MDCCCCXXXV (9060), fo. 1r-v. The title page (in Morone's hand) for a different work on 2304, fo. 172r makes against Dunn's contention that this was the MS sent Cardinal Contarini which then remained in Venice.

Introduction

Priuli and/or Binardi and at one point found in Rome, appeared in Perugia, before being returned in 1621 to the Vatican Library at Cardinal Scipione Cobelluzzi's request.[93] By then another large loss had befallen the codices. That everything else inventoried in ASV, Misc. Arm. II 79 is now in Vat. lat. 5964-72 makes it very likely that "De modo concionandi" was among those volumes at Pole's death, and therefore followed at least some of their itinerary. If this hypothesis is correct, the work had disappeared (at least as a distinct entity) by the time of Cobelluzzi's request. Napoleone Comitoli turned over to the Vatican the nine volumes of Pole's papers which presently survive, and which were then with the Barnabites of the College of Sant' Erculano, Perugia, Comitoli's bishopric.[94] Requests to transfer important treasures from the Papal States to Rome were common, so it may be that no particular significance attaches to Cobelluzzi's.[95] Then again, Cobelluzzi and Comitoli worked together in Rome on the *Congregatio interpretum Concilii Tridentini*, of which Comitoli was secretary, closely enough that Comitoli turned over to Cobelluzzi Cardinal Antonio Carafa's manuscript on the council which Comitoli had prepared for publication.[96] Carafa had been Comitoli's patron since the late 1570s when Carafa summoned Comitoli to Rome as his auditor, and after that he became Auditor of the Rota until 1587.[97] It may be that Comitoli's service to

---

[93] For Cobelluzzi see *DBI*, 26, pp. 433-5.

[94] Jeanne Bignami Odier, *La Bibliothèque Vaticane de Sixte IV a Pie XI. Recherches sur l'histoire des collections de manuscrits* (Vatican City: Biblioteca Apostolica Vaticana, 1973; Studi e Testi, 272), p. 107 and Pagano-Ranieri, pp. 51 and 52n, the chapter act of 2 November 1621.

[95] Giovanni Battista Vermiglioli, *Cenni storici sulle antiche biblioteche pubbliche di Perugia* (Perugia: Bartelli, 1843), pp. 46-47.

[96] Giovanni Papa, "Il cardinale Antonio Carafa prefetto della S. Congregazione del Concilio" in *La Sacra congregazione del concilio (1564-1964)* (Vatican City: no publisher, 1964), pp. 309-38, pp. 318-19 and Sebastian Tromp, "De manuscriptis acta et declarationes antiquas S. Congregationis Concilii Tridentini continentibus. Sectio altera," *Gregorianum*, 39 (1958): 93-120, pp. 111-12.

[97] Annibale Mariotti, *De' Perugini auditori della sacra rota romana. Memorie*

Carafa brought him the Pole MSS, and he was deeply involved in the disposition of Carafa's collection of conciliar materials.[98] Perhaps it is not a coincidence that Carafa died in 1591, the same year Comitoli moved to Perugia.

It seems almost certain that Comitoli brought the papers with him rather than having found them there upon his arrival. Only one of his immediate predecessors as bishop, Vincenzo Ercolani, had any obvious link to Pole or his circles.[99] It is remotely possible that Cardinal della Rovere, Pole's protégé as a youth, might have had a role in the transfer when he was vice-legate of Perugia, but there is no evidence to support that theory. That the papers came to the Barnabites once they got to Perugia was Comitoli's doing. He founded the house there in 1607, and granted it Pole's papers.[100] It is still a little obscure why the Barnabites should have wanted the codices, but it may simply be that Comitoli used the house as a secure depository. He made it the heir of his own papers.[101]

---

istoriche (Perugia: Carlo Baduel, 1787), p. 99.

[98] In his preface to Carafa's book, Comitoli noted that other of Carafa's MSS about Trent passed to his heirs, and that some were sold on the orders of Cardinal Mattei, Carafa's successor as prefect of the congregation. BAV, Vat. lat. 6326, fo. 1r-v. Papa, "Antonio Carafa," p. 319; Tromp, "De manuscriptis," p. 112; Bignami Odier, pp. 107 and 124. The rest of Carafa's MSS were apparently left to the BAV, including Vat. lat. 3454-3553, although his will has not been found; cf. Bignami Odier, pp. 70 and 83n2. BAV, Vat. lat. 3553 is a list of the donated MSS (Bignami Odier, p. 97n.104); fo. 22r has a note of various persons having other "pezzi" etc., following a list of MSS not handed over. BAV, Vat. lat. 3510 has a note on its flyleaf that it was given by Carafa's will. Another list of Carafa's MSS is Biblioteca Ambrosiana, Milan, H. 1. inf., fos. 266r-77r. Cf. Pagano-Ranieri, p. 51.

[99] In addition to Ercolani (died 1586), they were Cardinal Fulvio Corneo, Francesco Bosio, and Antonio Maria Galli. Conrad Eubel and J. Van Gulik, *Hierarchia catholica medii et recentioris aevii*, 3 (Münster: Bibliothek Regensberger, 1913), p. 272. For Ercolani and Pole, see ab. note 45.

[100] Orazio Premoli, *Storia dei Barnabiti nel Cinquecento* (Rome: Desclée, 1913), p. 383. Pagano-Ranieri, 52n.

[101] Mariotti, *Perugini auditori*, p. 107 and Vermiglioli, *Scrittori perugini*, pp. 333-4. A codicil added to Comitoli's will in 1623 confirming the Barnabites as

Introduction

Unfortunately, I have been unable to find any evidence that Comitoli's patron Carafa ever had the MSS. None of his correspondence mentions them, and unsurprisingly neither does the list of his MSS donated to the BAV.[102] Had he possessed them, they may have come from several sources. One may have been Cardinal Gabriele Paleotti, his satellite and co-worker on the congregation for Trent.[103] I base this supposition on the possibility that Paleotti at one time had Pole's papers, an educated guess resting on the appearance at the end of Vat. lat. 5966, fos. 212r-18r of a notarial copy of the will of Francesco Andrea de Casale, papal treasurer of Bologna, dated 20 July 1552. The notary was Benedetto Paleotti (fo. 218r). He must have been a relative of Cardinal Gabriele, since there was only one family of that name in Bologna and they were all lawyers and notaries. (One of the cardinal's grandfather's brothers was named Benedetto, for what that is worth.)[104] Or perhaps they came from

---

his heirs and putting that disposition into effect survives, but his wills of 1607 and 1610 have not been found. They are supposed already to have established the Barnabites as his legatees. Vermiglioli, *Scrittori perugini*, p. 334 citing "Lib. Testam." of Marco Torelli, 3, p. 68, now Archivio di Stato, Perugia, Notarile, Protocolli, no. 2661, fos. 68r-69r. I am grateful to the director of the Archivio for sending me a copy. The earlier wills may yet turn up among the forty-four volumes in Torelli's *notarili*, if not among the papers of another notary. Soprintendenza Archivistica per il Lazio, l'Umbria e le Marche, *Gli archivii dell'Umbria* (Rome, 1957; Pubblicazioni degli Archivii di Stato, 30), p. 46.

[102] According to the article on Carafa in the *DBI*, his correspondence is found in BAV, Barb. lat. 5698-5741 and 9920. I have seen all but the last, and these volumes are not exclusively or even mainly Cardinal Carafa's letters, but rather the largest single piece of the Carafa family archive, dating back to the mid-1550s with an occasional item earlier. Cardinal Carafa's correspondence consists only of in-letters, with one or two exceptions. It is found chiefly in volumes 5722-25 and 5727-39, together with 2150 (fos. 34-54); 5795, fo. 277; 3615, fos. 14-18; 3620, fo. 209; 5709; and 5711 (ten letters from Cardinals Santoro and Sirleto). According to the catalogue in the Sala consultazione of the BAV, Barb. lat. 5726, fos. 38-49 are letters from Antonio to his uncle Cardinal Carlo Carafa, but they are actually from one Antonia Carafa.

[103] E.g., BAV, Barb. lat. 5711, fo. 1r, a letter of 1574 from Paleotti to Carafa saying that the writer had executed Carafa's orders.

[104] Paolo Prodi, *Il cardinale Gabriele Paleotti (1522-1597)*, two volumes (Rome:

Morone, or from Seripando or some of the others involved in the Rome publication project, or perhaps from Cardinal Stanislaus Hosius. Hosius was one of the last legates to the council and involved in the *congregatio*'s founding, later serving on it from 1574 to 1579, and he owned a copy of the preface to *De unitate* addressed to Edward VI (catalogue no. 2).[105]

Whether Carafa had these volumes or Comitoli obtained them through other means, it seems most likely that they were extracted from the Inquisition's archive. The near certainty that one of the works now there (the preface to Edward VI noted above) was once part of the same numbering scheme as covers Vat. lat. 5964-72 points to that conclusion. Further, some of the notations on those codices, precisely identifying "fragmentum tertium" of "De reformatione ecclesiae," for example, could be the Inquisition's work.[106] By contrast, the acts of the *processo Morone* are much more heavily annotated, and the Pole materials in the ACDFSO have only one such note on them, which paradoxically seems to say that those works which most look because of their annotations as if they attracted the inquisitors' attention were never in their archives, while those that were certainly in the archive seem never to have attracted their attention. The identifications of hands on some of the texts also seem designed to help the inquisitors. The fluidity of the relations between Biblioteca apostolica and Archivio Castel Sant'Angelo in the late sixteenth and early seventeenth centuries probably extended to the Inquisition's archive. For instance, Tommaso Gualteruzzi's *processo*, which should have been in the Inquisition's possession, passed back and forth between the BAV and the Archivio.[107]

Edizioni di storia e letteratura, 1959-1967), p. 40n. I owe information about the family to Prodi.

[105] Sebastian Tromp, "De cardinalibus interpretibus S. Concilii Tridentini annis 1564-1600," in *La sacra congregazione*, pp. 251-63, pp. 254-55.

[106] BAV, Vat. lat. 5964, fo. 294r foot.

[107] ASV, Indice 19, fo. 36r, a list of "Libri di Castello dati a N[ostro]. S[ignore].," 11 February 1614, including "Libri sei in foglio appartenenti alla causa di Mons. Tomaso Gualterucci." Cf. Bignami Odier, pp. 103-5.

Introduction

Cobelluzzi was both archivist of Castel Sant'Angelo and cardinal librarian, as well as a member of the congregation of the Inquisition and then of Propaganda Fide thus his decision to add the volumes to the BAV and not to the archive in Castel Sant'Angelo, or even to that of the Holy Office, must mean that the Inquisition's interest in Pole had cooled rapidly. Perhaps the creation of the myth of "Catholic reform" covered enough sins by joining erstwhile *spirituali* with those like Alvise Contarini who might once have been their enemies.[108]

The numbering scheme may say a little about the history of the Vatican's holdings at this early period. Above all, it seems to indicate that the present arrangement of volumes postdates the numbering. Thus, for example, numbers 60bis and 62 are in Vat. lat. 5964, while nearly all the numbers up to 60 are in 5970, except for 39, found in 5971—the only numbered piece in that codex. By far the largest percentage of the numbers appear in Vat. lat. 5970, a total of 16 (see table). The distribution of the numbers indicates that losses occurred mainly at both ends of the series. The only numbers before 30 are 4, 6, 9, 10 and 12. Similarly, the only numbers above 62 are 79, 88, 97 and 100. Perhaps unsurprisingly, most of the numbered items are connected to *De unitate*. Some of the numbering seems intended to link similar works, perhaps in preparation for their publication. Thus no. 39 is the preface to Edward VI and nos. 40-41 are two versions of the *Apologia* to Charles V, as is no. 45, and nos. 46-47 are general prefaces. Nos. 43-44, which break into the sequence of texts linked to *De unitate*, are nevertheless two versions of *De summo pontifice*. The *De unitate* series continues through the fifties, including no. 50, the ACDFSO version of the preface to King Edward. Nos. 59-60 are two later texts concerning the reconciliation of England. Ten are marked "select:" one version of "De summo pontifice extra conclavi;" "In librum Actorum Apostolorum usque ad iii cap.;" "De passione Christi;" two prefaces to *De unitate*, to Charles V and the king of France; a set of instructions for a delegation to the emperor; Ormanetto's reply

---

[108] Fragnito, "Censura," p. 45.

to parliament; Pole's companion to the last; the reply to Richard Morison's *Invective against Treason*; and "Proposita a D. Carli. Paul iii de rebus Anglicis cum mitturus esset legatos de pace ad principes," which is not Pole's work. Although these would appear not to have been singled out for the same reasons, most of them might be linked as worthy of special examination for what they had to say about papal authority and how Pole had used it as a legate, allegedly the real reason for Paul IV's proceeding against him.[109] Were the numbers the work of the Inquisition, rather than of someone engaged in the publishing campaign? On the one hand, numbering sequestered documents was inquisitorial practice, although the best known case, the *processo* Morone, was apparently handled somewhat randomly.[110] On the other hand, all Pole's works in the ACDFSO except the preface to Edward VI do not have numbers, and, as we have seen, the numbered works unlike Morone's documents are only very sparingly annotated. Nevertheless, the possibility that the Inquisition's servants added the numbers cannot be excluded.

---

[109] Henri de Sponde, *Annalium emin'mi Cardinalis Caes. Baronii continuatio, ab anno M. C. XCVII...ad finem M. DC. XL* (Paris: Denis de la Noüe, 1641), p. 325.

[110] *PM*, 2, pp. 191-202. The notary Claude De Valle signed many more of these documents than he numbered.

Introduction

Table

Numbers appearing in Vat. lat. 5964-72 by codex

5964	2 (60bis and 62)
5965	2 (43-44, in fo. sequence)
5966	0
5967	0 (unsurprising, since this is a volume mainly of correspondence)
5968	3 (including a number, 97, which appears to refer to the whole volume; the others are 6 and 100)
5969	5 (4, 9-10 in folio sequence, 35 and 46bis)
5970	16 (30?, 40-41 in fo. sequence, 32, 37bis, 45-47 (in work series, but not folio), 52-53, 55-56, 56bis?, 59-60, 79)
5971	1 (39)
5972	1 (12)

Catalogue of Works

This catalogue is an attempt to describe in palaeographical and to the extent possible codicological terms the state of Pole's manuscripts. The object is to make available to researchers information that has never been collected, much less published. Given Pole's central importance in the history of the Reformation and how much has been said about his ideas with no or inadequate reference to the manuscripts, this catalogue when read in conjunction with my biography offers the first scientifically adequate foundation for interpretation. Neither is the final word, but it should be much easier to conduct further investigations with this catalogue in hand.

A word of caution about it. 1) A few works that exist only in printed texts have been included, but no attempt has been made to exhaust printed editions for which MSS survive. 2) It is not always possible to be certain which MS Querini published, given his habit of expurgating and sometimes polishing texts, and the failings of some of his amanuenses in transcribing the originals. 3) The works are in rough order of importance, since it is almost impossible to put them in a chronological sequence. 4) Most of the catalogues descend from Dudic's. Anthony à Wood's, for example, is virtually a quotation with a few bibliographical additions, and Dodd and Tanner took over nearly all of Wood.[111] 5) Numbers are added to entries in the earlier catalogues for convenience. 6) I have been more than usually cautious about identifying hands, given the notorious problems of distinguishing one Italic or Secretary from another, and have preferred to identify speculation as such rather than dignifying it as something more. It also appears that Pole's secretariate may have had a distinctive script, an adaptation of Italic, increasing the difficulties in identifying any individual hand.

---

[111] Joseph Gillow took his catalogue in large part from Dodd/Tootell, with the addition of a few printed editions. *A Literary and Biographical History or Biographical Dictionary of the English Catholics*, six volumes (London: Burns and Oates, 1885-1905), 5, pp. 339-40.

Catalogue of Works

1) *De unitate.*

ATTESTATIONS: Every catalogue of Pole's works includes his most famous, but only the printed editions. Tanner gives one of Rome, 1562, which must be a confusion for the Manuzio edition of *De concilio*, etc. (catalogue no. 16). In addition, Wood, no. 2; Dodd, no. 4; Tanner; and Klaiber, no. 2574 noted Vergerio's parody.

Probably the main text of two of these three, a) and b), is in the same hand, and possibly all three are, if allowance is made for a copyist writing at different speeds and under different circumstances.[112] BNM nevertheless appears to be in a different hand throughout, particularly on the grounds that the macrons in it are horizontal, while they are vertical in the other two texts.[113] In any case, they are all three in a very similar Italic, with a very similar slant. Vat. lat. and PRO seem to be in the same hand as Vat. lat. 5826, fo. 37r, a letter to Cardinal Contarini from Liège of July 1537 (cf. the minute in the same hand in Vat. lat. 5967, fos. 184r-85r) and probably Vat. lat. 5967, fo. 176r (another letter of similar date), and perhaps Vat. lat. 5826, fo. 32r (a fair copy of the letter in 5967, fo. 184r), which, however, contains a very distinctive macron-t which does not appear in the other hands. The hand has not been identified. It is probably not that of Bernardino Sandro, known to have been a copyist in Pole's household a little earlier.[114] His hand is established from another letter in Vat. lat. 5826, fo. 39r by comparision of its Greek hand to that of New College, Oxford, MS 31, fo. 17, by Bernardinus.[115]

---

[112] For the difficulty of achieving certainty, cf., for example, the main text of BNM, fo. 124r with the correction at its foot and BAV, Vat. lat. 5826, fo. 32r.

[113] Dunn, "Text," p. 456, thought there were five hands in BNM. Many points of his description need correction, but I am very grateful to him for the gift of his extensive collection of materials on the text.

[114] BL, Cotton Nero B VII, fo. 111v (*L&P*, 9, no. 512), to Thomas Starkey, 1 October 1535. His principal job seems to have been butler.

[115] E. Lobel, "Cardinal Pole's Manuscripts," *Proceedings of the British Academy*, 1931, pp. 97-101, plate 1. Sandro was famous as a Greek copyist. See *Reportorium der griechischen Kopisten 800-1600*, 1, Grossbritannien. A. *Verzeichnis der kopisten*, ed. Ernst Gamillscheg and Dieter Harlfinger (Vienna:

In addition to the apparent palaeographical evidence, the strongest argument against Sandro being the copyist of *De unitate* is that he was then involved in a different project.[116] Lily wrote a very similar Italic; cf Bodl. Library MS Broxbourne 84.11. If the texts in Vat. lat. 5826 and 5967, used for comparison, are not Sandro's work, they could have been written by one of the temporary members of Pole's household loaned by Giberti on their legation in 1537, including Trifone Benci and perhaps the mysterious Matteo Canossa. They are probably not in the hand of either Francesco della Torre or Adamo Fumano. See, for comparison, BAV, Barb. lat. 5095, fo. 205v (della Torre) and Barb. lat. 5695, fo. 45r (Fumano). In any case, none of these four is known to have been with Pole in 1536. Other possiblities include Goldwell.[117] It is also not beyond the realm of possibility that some or all of these texts are autograph. The difficulty in establishing that proposition is that all those roughly contemporary texts known to be autograph, perhaps especially Vat. lat. 5970, fos. 303r-12r which dates from 1539, are drafts and much more quickly written than any of the texts of *De unitate*.

MSS:
   a) Vat. lat. 5970.1, fos. 1-125. Title (fo. 1r): "Libri 4or ad Henricum Regem Cum Adnotationes Domini Danielis." Fair copy with corrections. Foliated (upper right) and sigillated (lower right). Gatherings of twelve. Fo. 125r is headed "Correcta et annotata per D. Danielem Penitentiarum in 4o libros ad Henricum" and fo. 150v reads "Annota per D. Danielem," as if docketed. Thomas F. Dunn mistakenly said that the MS was "prepared *per*

Austrian Academy of Sciences, 1981), no. 39.

[116] BL, Cotton Nero B VII, fo. 125r-v.

[117] For Lily, see W. G. Zeeveld, *Foundations of Tudor Policy* (Cambridge, Mass.: Harvard University Press, 1948), pp. 97-98, corrected by my entry in *New DNB*; for Goldwell, A. B. Emden, *A Biographical Register of the University of Oxford A. D. 1501 to 1540* (Oxford: Oxford University Press, 1974) and my *New DNB* entry.

Danielem Penitentiarum."[118] Daniel's identity is unknown, and it is unclear whether any of the corrections to the printed edition in 5970 are his, especially since Francisco de Navarra is also known to have sent corrections.[119] There are three sets: fos. 127r-150r (cf. fo. 126v "Correttioni del libro stampato di Monsignore" as if docketed, except upside down for filing, and in lower right corner, upside down:"88 correti. librorum imprimorum (?)"); fos. 151r- 53r, a sequentially numbered series of corrections, keyed to page, not folio numbers; and fo. 154r, an incomplete set, keyed 51-60, probably intended to fill a gap between fos. 151v/152r. This last set does not fit the 1539 edition, Vat. lat., PRO nor BNM text, but may perhaps refer to Vergerio's Strasbourg edition in folio, which nonetheless had page numbers.

b) PRO, SP 1/104, pages 1-280. Fair copy with autograph corrections. The dating clause is probably autograph.

c) BNM, Ms. Lat. IV, 114 (2304), fos. 1r-171v.[120] Title (fo. 1r): "Cardinalis Poli de Auctoritate Rom. Pontificis Adversus Anglicanam Ecclesiam." Corrections in perhaps two or three other hands, including Pole's. Collation: fo. 2r "A" upper left corner; fo. 14r "B" and cross at head, continued to fo. 25v; fo. 26r "C" and cross, continued 26v-7r, 28r-29r, large cross at head rectos fos. 30r-33r; fo. 34r "D;" fo. 40r "E;" from fos. 44r-46r also numbered 5r-7r; fo. 52r "F" aft. del. "D," numbered also 1r-22r thru fo. 73r; fo. 73r has note at foot next to triangle with "x" through it "v. p. 74"; fo. 73v has large device in left margin mid-page with note "v. pag. 77" (cross-reference on fo. 77v foot); fo. 74r "G;" fo. 78r numbered over 23; fo. 78v has device in left margin mid-page with note "v. p. 79" (cross-reference at head fo. 79r); fo. 80v has note at foot "V. continuas p. 95 ad hoc signum," a long "f" with double cross-bar (cross-reference on fo. 95r); fos. 81r-95r have long horizontal lines with two parallel vertical strokes at both head and foot of every page; fos 81r-83r over 24r-26r; fo. 84r "G" aft. del. "E;" fo. 100r "H;" fo. 116r "I" aft. del. "G;" fo. 132r "L"

---

[118] Dunn, "Text," p. 458.

[119] *CRP*, no. 604.

[120] Dunn, "Text," p. 456 gave the incorrect *segnatura* of VIII, 3 (2304).

aft. del. "h" and "H;" fo. 148r "M;" fo. 164r "N." Fos. 173r-85v are additions to the MS, together with another copy of the conclusion; fo. 180r "G," and that folio may be in another hand. Fo. 172r is a title page, perhaps in the hand of the title on Vat. lat. 5969, fo. 314r (Morone's?): "Dell'officio del sommo Pontifice lib. 5 [*ov.* 4] scritti fuori di conclavi No. 37 [*aft. del.* 18]. Copia piu corretta. il primo libro è in mano di ms. Alvigi Contarino. il 2.o anchora s'è dato al medesimo." There is a note at the bottom of the page in a different hand: "N. B. Haec folii continent fragmentum operis Reginaldi Poli S. R. E. Cardinali, pro Ecclesiasticis Unitatis Defensione, quod ipse auctor reputavit, ut apparet ex signaturis in Codice, qui totum opus complectitur. Numeri in fronte cuiusque folii responderit numeris foliorum integri Codicis."[121]

EDITIONS:

a) Rome: Antonio Blado, [1539] (reprinted: Farnborough, Hants.: Gregg Press, 1965);[122]

b) Strasbourg: Wendelin Rihelius, 1555;

c) Ingolstadt: David Sartorius, 1587, which on sig. 4r-[8v] reprints Manuzio's preface to *De concilio*;[123]

d) Rocaberti, pp. 191-311;

e) partially published as *Oratio. . .qua Caesaris. . .conatur. . . inflammare, ut adversum eos, qui nomen Evangelio dederunt, arma sumat. . . cum Scholiis Athanasii* [i. e., Pierpaolo Vergerio]

---

[121] There may well be lost MSS of *De unitate*, created in 1553 and 1554 when Pole was under heavy pressure to republish the work. See ab., pp. 21-22, 25. Then again, the lack of any later MSS may mean that he never got far in bowing to that pressure, despite writing at least one preface for a new edition. See catalogue, no. 2.

[122] The date of the edition is established by a marginal note treating Cromwell as still alive (fo. LXXXVIII) and Pole's reference to finding *De unitate* in print, divided into books and without a preface on his return from Spain, that is, in 1539. *ERP*, 1, p. 344.

[123] Paolo Simoncelli, *Il caso Reginald Pole: eresia e santità nelle polemiche religiose del cinquecento* (Rome: Edizioni di storia e letteratura, 1977), p. 217 identified this as a new preface. It is almost entirely reprinted in Alfonso Chacón, ed. Agostino Oldoino, *Vitae et res gestae pontificum romanorum et S. R. E. cardinalium ab initio nascentis ecclesiae usque ad Clementem IX P. O. M.* (Rome: P. and A. De Rubeis, 1677), cc. 639-41.

(Venice, 1554); Pole referred in a letter to Cardinal Truchsess of 20 June 1554 [*CRP*, no. 885] to this translation as having been sent to him from Rome, so the publication must predate June by some time) and translated as *The seditious and Blasphemous Oration of Cardinal Pole, translated into English by Fabian Wythers* (London: O. Rogers, 1560; STC no. 20087). Marie Hallé thought the copy in the British Library had been published during Pole's lifetime, but gave no bibliographical evidence.[124]

TRANSLATIONS:

a) Pole's Defense of the Unity of the Church, trans. and intro. Joseph G. Dwyer (Westminster, Md.: Newman Press, 1965);

b) Défense de l'unité de l'église, ed. Noëlle Marie Egretier (Paris: J. Vrin, 1967).

d) Vergerio's translation of the appeal to Charles V: Thüringisches Hauptstaatsarchiv, Weimar, Reg. N. 749, fos. 1r-11v.[125] It dates the text from which the translation was taken 1554 ("Ausgetzogenn aus seinnen bucher in welche er geschrieben hatt zu beschirmen die einigkeit der kirchen anno 1554"), which must mean that it translates Vergerio's *Oratio* (bel.), and not part of *De unitate*.

2) Preface to *De unitate* addressed to Edward VI.

DATE:

This preface was probably begun in approximately 1552, since Pole said he thought it especially appropriate to write when Edward, *adolescentiam ingrediens*, found himself at Hercules's crossroads, and when the nuncio in France thought he saw an opening in England.[126] The second edition of Nicholas Sander, *De*

---

[124] Marie Hallé, *Life of Reginald Pole*, written under the pseudonym of Martin Haile (London: Pitman, 1911; originally published 1910), p. 344. Hallé may have been drawing on Cooper, I, p. 185, which gave the date of 1554.

[125] I owe this information to my former student, Peter Elsel Starenko.

[126] ACDFSO, fo. 29v; ASAS, 40/76, fo. 24r; *ERP*, 4, p. 346. *Correspondance du nonce en France Prospero Santa Croce (1552-1554)*, intro. by Francesco Giannetto, ed. J. Lestocquoy (Rome: Gregorian University Press, 1972; Acta Nuntiaturae Gallicae, 9), no. 32.

origine ac progressu schismatis anglicani, libri tres. . .aucti per Edouardum Rishtonum (Rome: Bartolomeo Bonfadini, 1586), p. 244, made it appear that Pole commenced work about the time he was at Trent, perhaps in late 1546, and added it as a fifth book to the rest of *De unitate* in Viterbo, apparently shortly before the conclave of Julius III (p. 309). Pole may have begun to write seriously only in the summer of 1554, according to a letter of early 1555 to Truchsess.[127] In the letter, Pole referred to Truchsess's deter-mined efforts to induce him to publish. Pole relented on that score, but continued work after Vergerio's edition was published. No edition of that preface is known. This preface also refers to Truchsess's pressure on Pole. Then again, the correspondence with Truchsess may not refer to this preface, since Truchsess urged Pole to explain what the oration to Charles V contained in *De unitate* was meant to do in response to Vergerio's *Oratio*, and the preface to Edward does not do that. No other known work seems more likely, however, and none of the prefaces to *De unitate* addresses the oration, either.

ATTESTATIONS: Dudic, no. 2; Wood, no. 6; Tanner; Klaiber, no. 2584 (from Schelhorn).

MSS:
a) ACDFSO, St St. E-6-a fasc. 3: "Proemium ad Eduardum VI angliae Regem in 4. libros ad Henricum octavum eius patrem scriptos de unitate ecclesiae duo exemplaria [crossed out in pencil] N. 41 [crossed out in ink and replaced with 50]." Thirty-four folios in either Faita's or Dudic's hand, with corrections, not autograph. First page numbered at head 67, corrected from 66. Incipit (hereafter In.): "Etsi multa me hoc tempore, ne ad te scribam, Princeps, dehortantur." Explicit (hereafter Ex.): "Nunc ad quae ad patrem tuum scripsi, mentem iam, si placet, cogitationemque converte."

b) ASAS, 40/76, in Faita's hand.

c) BCQ, MS F. III. 7, m. 1, fos. 88r-126v. Headed in different hand from main text: "Eduardo Henrici filio Angliae Regi Reginaldus Cardinalis Polus. S." Separate collation of 1-39 in upper

---

[127] *CRP*, no. 1034.

right corner (probably eighteenth-century). Described on possibly original table of contents and on modern title page for this piece as "Imperfecta." Fair copy, perhaps in Holland's hand, with two corrections outside the line of writing. Also some *pentimenti* of no importance, e.g., relatively frequent errors in case and one infinitive given a final "m," or a tag on a recto, in the copyist's hand. The presence of a marginal note in the same unknown but contemporary hand on this and ASAS, 40/76 proves their close relationship in time.

Querini appeared to claim that he got his text from that printed in 1737 by Johann Georg Schelhorn, but a collation of Querini's text against ACDFSO, St. st. E-6-a, fasc. 3 demonstrates that Querini's version is much closer to it than to BCQ, MS F. III. 7, m. 1, Schelhorn's MS, which Querini alleged was the only one extant.[128] The incipit in BCQ, to cite one simple example, is missing the "ne" contained in both *ERP* and ACDFSO. If Querini, the cardinal librarian, did have access to the Inquisition's archives, it must have been at the price of the same kind of silence imposed on De Luca.

Schelhorn later sent Querini his MS, apparently the whole volume rather than just this preface, since other pieces of it are now to be found in the BCQ.[129] For example, Schelhorn cited Cardinal Hosius's judgment of the ministries of Heidelberg and Zürich, which is BCQ, MS D. II. 18, including Hosius's autograph covering letter. There are probably other pieces there as well, headed in the library's catalogue "Tridentinum Concilium," but I was unable to consult them. All the pieces I could see have separate gold paper covers, which seem to have been the work of the owner before Schelhorn. He traced the codex's provenance back to Hosius, via the catalogue of Johann Friedrich Mayer. Mayer got it from Charles XII of Sweden after his war against Poland. It was cited in Mayer's catalogue as "Volumen actorum Concilii Tridentini," some of which were in Hosius's hand. Each

---

[128] *ERP*, p. xxxiv. J. G. Schelhorn, *Amoenitates historiae ecclesiasticae et litterariae* (Frankfurt and Leipzig: Daniel Bartholomäus, 1737), pp. 192-276. The discussion here of the manuscripts and their provenance supersedes that in "Sticking-Plaster Saint," p. 216.

[129] *ERP*, 4, p. 353.

piece in the codex was bound singly by Bishop Uffenbach, who bought it from Mayer, before reselling it to Schelhorn in 1726. Schelhorn further discovered that it had once been in the library of Johann Burchard Mencken, and then migrated to that of Heinrich de Bunau.[130]

d) Vat. lat. 5970.2, fos. 388-95v. Title on fo. 386r: no. 52 "Fragmentum scripti ad Regem Eduardum." In.: "Cum hic nulla alia de causa, divinae legis velamen desiderio suo superposuit." Ex.: "Quo pacto deus hanc tam gravem hypocrisim castigavit." Vat. lat. 5971:

e) fos. 1br-57v [no.] 39. "Scripta ad Eduardum VI quod addit D. Card.is post libros 4or ad Henricum eius patrem," in same hand as an illegible title in Vat. lat. 5970, towards end; body of text fair copy with some autograph corrections. Possibly same hand as first version "De reformatione ecclesiae"; cf. version on fos. 117r-149v. In.: "Si me, tu, nunc princeps, vel me ipsum defendentem, contra iniquorum." Ex.: "cum post illud tempus quo ab ecclesia defecit, et paulo," and half page then deleted.

f) fos. 89r-114v. Mostly illegible because of brown paper. Probably another version. In.: illegible. Ex.: "expectarem si digna praemiis me facisse onderem rem."

g) fos. 117r-149v. Mainly legible, but brown paper throughout. Separate pagination 1-34. Cf. fair copy on fos. 1br-57v. In.: "Si me tu nunc princeps vel me ipsum defendentem contra iniquorum calumnias." Ex.: "omnis qui amoris (?) sensu cavent sic quidem," a tag?, but del. Cf. fo. 115r-v: In.: "Si me vel in iis quae ad te scripsi Princeps, quae meam contra iniquorum calumnias." Ex.: "si digna praemiis me fecisse onderem."

h) There are probably other fragments of these or other versions in this volume, e.g., on fos. 65r-86r. In.: "sed qua propius illum ad interitum suum accedere videbam eo magiori studio exarsisse servandi eum." Ex.: "primi homini cui omnibus dotibus naturae ornato hortum in eodem plantaverat."

EDITIONS:

a) Johann Georg Schelhorn, *Amoenitates historiae ecclesiasticae et litterariae,* two volumes (Frankfurt and Leipzig: Daniel

---
[130] *Amoenitates,* pp. 187-88.

Bartholomäus, 1737), 1, pp. 192-276; b) *ERP*, 4, pp. 306-53.

3) Other prefaces to *De unitate*.

ATTESTATIONS: none.

MSS:
Vat. lat. 5970.2:
To the king of Scotland:

DATE: Perhaps roughly contemporary with no. 4, on the grounds of similar content.

a) fos. 184r-189v. Title on fo. 183r: "Prohemio del libro del Rmo Polo al Re d'Inghilterra" (rest of folio blank). Breaks off in mid-sentence and mid-page on fo. 189v. Fair copy. In.: "Quo magis mecum considero, inclite Rex, quam facile." Ex.: "Hic ergo plus oculis credi, quam auribus, plus factis quam verbis est necesse." Fair divergences between this version and the next appear at, e.g., the top of *ERP*, p. 175 where the material is heavily rearranged, although largely identical for content, and *ERP* breaks off probably somewhere on fo. 188v.[131]

b) fos. 284r-289v mid-page. Draft, with widely spaced lines and probably autograph corrections. No. 53. In.: "Quo magis mecum consideram incliti Rex, quam facile." Ex.: "Si ergo licet indignum agnoscat qui principis sese rebus immisceat, tamen [*del.*]."

EDITION:
ERP, 1, pp. 172-78.

To the king of France:
DATE: Probably coeval with the last.

c) fo. 277r. "Ad Regem Gallorum de Rege Henrico imperfectum [marked for deletion], Duo exemplaria Imperfecta.

---

[131] Dunn, "Text," pp. 467-8 briefly considered this and two other texts in BAV, Vat. lat. 5970, fos. 278-83 and 284-99, calling them all versions of the preface to James V. That on fos. 278-83 seems rather to be to the king of France.

56 [*del.*]; No 46 [*del.*] 54; Select (mid-page)."

d) fos. 278r-83v. This looks very similar to the last. Fair copy with a few corrections. In.: "Quo magis mecum considere, Inclyte Rex, quam facile vicini tibi Regis." Ex.: "quod videlicet ab exemplo nectitur, quod maxime in," text which appears on fo. 189r a few lines from the end.

e) fos. 290r-99r. New text, but perhaps similar subject matter to last. Brown paper. In.: "Cum Regem (?) et sollicium (?)" Ex.: "Prestet ad hanc excutiendam promptiorem aditum habeamus. Nec enim."

To the reader:
DATE: unknown.

f) fos. 315r-328v (mid-page). Title on fo. 314r: "Praefatio [*ab. del.* "?"] ad lectorem;" cf. fo. 315r: "te admonitum volui Christiane lector. Qua te tuetur in editione libri ad Henricum viii. no. 47 ["7" *ov.* "0"]. 51 (?)" Probably in Holland's hand, with autograph corrections. In.: "Cum librum a me aliquot ante annos scriptum essem aediturus." Ex.: "eum non amplius cum natura nostra communicare."

4) "Apologia ad Carolum Quintum" (Querini's title).

ATTESTATION:
Klaiber, no. 2581 (Louvain, 1569, perhaps with *De summo pontifice*?; Ingolstadt, 1587, but this is probably a mistake for the section of *De unitate* addressed to Charles).

DATE:
1539, during Pole's second legation to the emperor. The clearest indication of its date comes in Pole's reference to having written *De unitate* "ante tertium annum" (*ERP*, 1, p. 75). It was intended as a preface to that work (*ERP*, 1, p. 75: "Omnia tunc scripta, quae nunc edo;" 78: "Cum haec tunc scriberem. . .in sequenti libro ante triennium scripta, ostendit;" and 80: "volui hunc librum, qui iram Dei erga Regem explicabit. . .quam alterum, in quo ejus sententia argumentis confutatur, praecedere." Paul Van Dyke

dated the "Apology" just before or during Pole's second legation, probably between March and September 1539. As he points out, Pole's reading of Richard Morison's *Invective against Treason* (published on 9 January), referred to in the "Apology" (*ERP*, 1, p. 113), provides another *terminus ad quem*.[132] As with all of Pole's writings, however, the likelihood is strong that he continued to work on it well after its original conception. The draft preface (ab. cat-alogue no. 3f) says *De unitate* had been written three years previously. This was later changed to five, so Pole must have continued to plan his own edition even after the Blado appeared.

MSS:
Vat. lat. 5970.2:

a) fos. 193r-235v. Fair copy with corrections. In.: "Grave est Caesar cor homini non." Ex.: "cum deo patre et sancto spirito sit sempiterna gloria HONOR DECUS ET IMPERIUM, per infinita seculorum secula. AMEN."

b) fos. 239r-268v. Title on fo. 238r: "[no.] 41, Exemplum imperfectum se[d?] correctum Apologiae super quatuor libris de unitate ecclesiae ad Henricum viii." Perhaps in Holland's hand, with corrections in secretary's hand and some autograph, but much of the text nearly a fair copy. Close to *ERP* through p. 136 l. 6 top, but not identical (e.g., explicit). In.: "Grave est Caesar, homini non maligno." Ex.: "scripsere magis ascultarem. Quid plura (?) Cum me" (no tag).
EDITION: *ERP*, 1, pp. 66-171.

c) fos. 303r-12r, autograph draft, probably an alternative version, which roots the origin of the "Apologia" in an audience with the emperor in Toledo in February 1539.[133]

d) "Historica expositio causae quae motus fuit Reginaldus Polus ad scribendum Henrico Octavo Angliae Regi quandam

---

[132] Paul van Dyke, "Reginald Pole and Thomas Cromwell: An Examination of the *Apologia ad Carolum Quintum*," *American Historical Review*, 9 (1904): 696-724, p. 703. For Pole's legation, see *Prince and Prophet*, chapter two.

[133] *CRP*, no. 242.

libellum" (Vat. lat. 12909, fo. 26r) once in the Beccadelli archive in Bologna, is probably a copy of the "Apologia" which Beccadelli had gotten when with Pole on his legation of 1539. It seems now to be lost.

5) "Oratio ab Henrico rege exercenda ad Deum" (title in later hand).

ATTESTATION: none.

DATE: unknown.

MS: Vat. lat. 5970.1, fos. 155r-181v. Fair copy, numbered at head 30.
EDITION: Dunn intended to publish this piece (there is a typescript transcription of it among the papers he gave me) but did not succeed.

6) On church property.

ATTESTATIONS: In addition to no. 34 below, there are two possibilities for the text vaguely referred to by Rullo on 25 May 1555 (De Frede, p. 67) and equally vaguely inventoried in ASV, Misc. Arm. II 79, fo. 363r, no. 7 ("Un trattato de bonis ecclesiasticis non usurpandis"). Dudic, no. 8 was more specific and the text he meant can be nearly precisely identified ("Libellus de restituendis Ecclesiae bonis, ad Philippum, & Mariam, Angliae Reges") as one of the first two entries; cf. Wood no. 11 (to Philip and Mary, n. d.); Tanner ("Of restoring the goods to the church, lib. 1. Written to K. Philip and Q. Mary").

MSS (of first possibility):

DATE: 22 December 1553.

a) Vat. lat. 5970.2, fos. 355r-66v. Title on fo. 354r: "De regno Angliae ad unitatem ecclesiae revocando ad Dominos de parliamento scriptus libellus ex itinerum cum legatus in Angliam ea de causa proficisceretur (?). No. 59. Select."

b) Vat. lat. 5968, fos. 107r(108r)-27r. "Another copye of a letter sent to the lordes spirituall & temporall in the firste perliament of quene marye concerning the realmes return to the obedience of the churche." A fair copy of a draft on fos. 87r(88r)-94v in Secretary hand, with a few corrections & additions. Indexed as "Oratio ad concilium parlamentum. Exemplaria duo." The partial overlap between this text and the harangue to Philip and Mary may explain why only "De bonis" was noticed in Dudic. Then again perhaps Binardi meant by the "Oratio" the text on fos. 305r-59r "Ad concilium parliamenti," a scribal copy (reading text?) of the speech given after Bishop Gardiner's on 28 November 1554. There is an autograph draft on fos. 129r-45v and fos. 361r-76v. Cf. a related text in *CRP*, no. 777 (summary).

c) ASV, Bolognetti 94, fos. 213r-18r.

d) Biblioteca Corsiniana, 33 E 19, pp. 400-10.

e) BL, Add. MS 25425, fos. 126r-9v.

EDITIONS: *ERP*, 5, pp. 157-71; *CRP*, no. 778 (summary).

MSS (of second possibility):

DATE: probably late 1554.

a) Vat. Lat. 5968, fos. 205r-226r, endorsed at foot to Somerset when governor of Edward, but actually to Philip and Mary. Indexed by Binardi at front of volume as "De bonis ecclesiasticis instituendis ad Philippum et Mariam reges, libellus ex latino in Anglicum conversus."
EDITION: *CRP*, no. 1010 (summary).

b) Vat. lat. 5968, fos. 69r-85v. Title: "A fragmente towching the disposition of the goodes of the churche." Draft in Secretary hand. Probably an alternative to a).
EDITION: *CRP*, no. 1009 (summary).

7) ***De sacramento.***

ATTESTATIONS: De Frede, pp. 67, 78, 100; Bernardo Navagero to

Doge and Senato (ASVe, Archivio Proprio Roma, 10, fo. 61v; *CSPV*, 6:2, no. 945; partially printed in *PM*, 5, "Documenti," no. 35); ASV, Misc. Arm. II 79, fo. 363r, no. 6; Tanner (*De eucharistia ad Cranmerum*, from Strype); Cooper (citing the 1584 edition); Klaiber, no. 2583.

DATE: Rullo referred to some version of this work in May 1555.[134] It may well have been reworked after Cranmer's trial reopened on 12 September, since its attack on Cranmer's perjury could have been intended as a reply to the defense that anyone swearing to both canon and common law must commit perjury to one, and perjury was one of the main charges against Cranmer.[135] Sometime before 26 October Pole sent the work to Muzzarelli.[136] Jaspar Ridley said it was written at Maguzzano (supposedly according to Strype) and sent to Cranmer on 23 October 1555 (apparently on the basis of *CRP*, no. 1415), but there is no evidence in favor of that location, nor was Pole there any longer in the summer of 1554, the alleged date of composition.[137] Stephen Gardiner, Lord Chancellor of England, may have ordered that the writing be translated into English and published.[138] According to Ludovico Castelvetro, Binardi translated *De sacramento* into Latin.[139]

---

[134] De Frede, p. 67.

[135] Diarmaid MacCulloch, *Thomas Cranmer. A Life* (New Haven and London: Yale University Press, 1996), pp. 576 and 578.

[136] *CRP*, no. 1415. Muzzarelli sent the letter back, but his comments are lost. *CRP*, no. 1439.

[137] Jasper Ridley, *Thomas Cranmer* (Oxford: Clarendon Press, 1962), p. 382, citing the 1840 edition of John Strype, *Memorials of the Most Reverend Father in God Thomas Cranmer*, p. 549, but this is an incorrect reference.

[138] As Brown (*CSPV*, 6:1, no. 255) translated, followed by Richard Watson Dixon, *History of the Church of England from the Abolition of the Roman Jurisdiction*, 4, *Mary-A. D. 1553-1558* (London: George Routledge and Sons, 1891), p. 425 and David Loades, *The Oxford Martyrs* (London: B. T. Batsford, 1970), p. 223, but the syntax is not entirely clear that Gardiner's order applied to whichever writing Pole had sent. See *CRP*, no. 1415.

[139] "Racconto delle vite," op. cit.

Catalogue of Works

MSS:

a) BL, Harleian 417, fos. 49r-68v. "Reginaldi Poli Cardinalis Legati apostolici epistola ad Thomam Cranmerum, qui Archipalem. sedem cantuarien. ecclesiae tenens, novam de sacramento Eucharistiae doctrinam contra perpetuum catholicae ecclesiae consensum professus est, ac tradidit, qua epistola eum nec magistrum tanti mysterii, neque discipulum idoneum esse posse; simulque unde hic eius error manarit, ostendit; et ad poenitentiam hortatur." Draft (but perhaps intended as fair copy, since it has tags) in Faita's hand with autograph corrections and probably some in Binardi's hand (e.g., fo. 20r). Incomplete. Collation: Originally foliated 1-20. R. W. Dixon said the letter ends with the autograph passage "The very truth comfort you in God, you not refusing his grace," but this is a mistake for the closing of Pole's letter of 6 November, which he signed as "Your very true comforter in God, you not refusing his grace."[140]

b) Vat. lat. 5967, fos. 141r-7v. "De Sacramento Eucharistiae Ad Thom. Cranmerum," numbered 48 on cover. Fair copy in Faita's hand in octavo.

c) PBN, MS lat. 6056, fos. 38v-70v, formerly Bib. Regiae 10213. "Reginaldi Poli Cardinalis. . .Epistola ad Thomam Cranmerum. . .de sacramento eucharistie. . .et ad penitentiam hortatur." In.: "Omnis qui recedit et non permanet in doctrina Christi deum non habet. Qui permanet in doctrina eius patrem et filium habent." Ex.: "agnosceas simulque intelligas quantopere emensa Christi misericordia indigeas ad quam ipse te Christus par [sic] me nnc [sic] invitat cuius voci [sic] quid respondere maximo cum desiderio tuae salutis expecto." Whole volume ruled off. Many *manicipii*, some marginal corrections. In same hand throughout. Original foliation, except for blank folios at end. MS cut down by at least one-half inch on top edge. Provenance: (foot fo.1r) "This booke was founde in my house amongst doctor Harpsfelds writings. William Carter." "John Hill" (probably signature) in pencil in top right corner of fo. 72r. The MS is almost certainly by Harpsfield. The Catholic printer Carter told Thomas Norton that, and Norton's description of the manuscript matches the BN

---

[140] Dixon, *Church of England*, p. 425n.

copy exactly.[141] James Gairdner assigned it to Alan Cope, working on a commission from Pole.[142] The reference to Harpsfield and his erudition on p. 23, cited by Gairdner, p. vii is explained by the identification device at the end of the MS, the same as that in Harpsfield's *Dialogi sex,* "AHLNHEVEAC," which John Pitts identified as meaning "Auctor huius libri Nicolaus Harpsfeldus. Eum vero edidit Alanus Copus."[143] Thus it was Cope who added praise of Harpsfield's learning, not unseemly hubris on Harpfield's part.

d) LPL, MS 2007, fos. 245-58. In.: "Omnis qui credit et non permanet in doctrina Christi, Deum non habet." Ex.: "ipsum e terris sustulisti, cuius peccati magnitudinem, et gravitatem utinam plane agnoscas, atque intelligas quantopere immensa Christi misericordiam indigas, ad quam ipse Christus per me nunc invitat, cuius voci quid respondeas maximo cum desiderio tuae salutis expecto." Probably a seventeenth-century copy, once sewn together as a separate booklet. MS 2007 was among the Fairhurst papers, bought by James Fairhurst shortly before World War II. They had been removed from Lambeth by John Selden in the seventeenth century, and were seen in the interval only by George Harbin in the eighteenth.[144]

e) Fragments in Vat. lat. 5968, fos. 227r-56v. Title: "A fragment towchinge the sacrament of the altare." Secretary hand (same as that on fos. 277ff?) with autograph corrections. In.: "and to be instructed in the truth." Ex.: "But these men will matter?" [as tag]. New heading on fo. 235r, but text continuous, including tag. Fos. 248r-56v entitled "Of the sacrament of the altare." Secretary hand with a few corrections. This item was incorrectly identified by Rex Pogson as having to do with the London synod. Instead, it is instructions almost certainly aimed at either

---

[141] BL, Add. MS 48029, fos 58r-9v. Cf. more cautiously MacCulloch, *Cranmer,* pp. 584-85.

[142] *Bishop Cranmer's Recantacyons* (London: Privately Printed, 1877), pp. viii-ix.

[143] De illustribus Angliae scriptoribus (1619), cited in E. Michael Camilli, "Six dialogues, 1566: Initial Response to the *Magdeburg Cen-turies,*" *Archiv für Reformationsgeschichte,* 86 (1995): 141-52, p. 142.

[144] E. G. W. Bill, *A Catalogue of Manuscripts in Lambeth Palace Library. MSS 1907-2340* (Oxford: Clarendon Press, 1976), pp. 29-30.

Catalogue of Works

Archdeacon Harpsfield alone, or all of Pole's commissioners for heresy.[145] They overlap to a great extent with the content of *De sacramento*, but do not show many textual connections.

EDITIONS:

a) Reginaldi Poli. Cardinalis Epistola de Sacramento Eucharistiae nunc primum in lucem edita opera Deodati Quistri Cremonensis (Cremona: Cristoforo Dracono, 1584);[146] b) Extracts of PBN, MS Lat. 6056 printed in *Recantacyons*, pp. 36-43; *c)* Ecclesiastical History Society, *Strype's memorials of archbishop Cranmer* (Oxford: James Wright, 1854; 3 vols), 3 pp. 614-44; *d) CRP*, no. 1411 (summary).

Transcripts of the edition: a) BCQ, G. V. 1, unfoliated; b) BNM, MS Zanetti 499 (1742), fos. 28r-54v, 55r-9v blank. Title: "Reginaldi Poli Card. Legati Apostolici Epistola ad Thomam Cranmerum, qui Archiespiscopalem Cantuariensis Ecclesiae tenens, novam de Sacramento Eucharistiae doctrinam contra perpetuae[um Catholicae] ecclesiae consensum professus est, ac tradit; Qua epistola eum nec magistrum tanti mysterii neque discipulum idoneum esse posse, simulque unde hic eius error manerit ostendit, ac ad poenitentiam hortatur." From Giacomo Contarini, apparently for whom was Codex CCCCXCIX. The volume includes many things of Cardinal Agostino Valier's, among them an original *gratulatio* to Pietro Francesco Contarini, Patriarch [probably of Aquileia] and a funeral oration for a doge. Most pieces set out with title pages in same hand, but not "De sacramento," probably because already had title. Fair copy in small Italic.

It is also possible that Zanetti 499 is not a transcript, but rather a copy of the MS from which the edition was taken, which may mean that the Venetian Valier may have had a hand in the publication. A partial collation of this MS with the edition

---

[145] Rex H. Pogson, "Cardinal Pole—Papal Legate to England in Mary Tudor's Reign," University of Cambridge, PhD. thesis, 1972, p. 203. Mayer, *Prince and Prophet*, chapt. 7 and *CRP*, no. 2208.

[146] The printer was among the first Italians to use Hebrew characters and responsible for the first edition of Tasso's *Aminta*, as well as the synodal acts of Cremona for 1604. Francesco Robolotti, *Cremona e sua provincia* (Cremona: No Publisher, 1839), pp. 325-26 and BAV card catalogue.

indicates that they are probably identical, but both vary, sometimes substantially, from a). Valier had many links to Pole's circles, as revealed by his biography of Pole's strong partisan Bernardo Navagero (sometime Venetian ambassador to Rome and then cardinal), in addition to his praise of Pole's ally Pietro Francesco Contarini. He also played a leading role in the congregation of the index from 1587, and wrote on how properly to publish books.[147]

TRANSLATIONS:
J. LeGrand, *Histoire du divorce de Henri VIII* (Paris: E. Martin, J. Bondot, and E. Martin, 1688), 1, pp. 289ff; reprinted in *ERP*, 5, pp. 238-74; re-translated in *Send-Schreiben dess Cardinals und Legaten dess apostolischen Stuhls Reginaldi Poli an Thomas Cranmer, Ertzbischoff zu Cambridge [sic] in Engelland, betreffend des Glaubens Punct. dess hochwürdigsten Sacraments dess Altars. Aus dem Frantzosischen in da Teutsche übersetzt* (Leipzig: Franz Anton Graf von Sporck, 1711).

8) "Della reforma"/"De reformatione ecclesiae."

ATTESTATIONS: Perhaps Marcantonio Da Mula to Seripando, Brussels, 23 August 1554 (BNN, MS XIII. AA. 57, fo. 23), saying that he and others had read Pole's treatise on the office of a good pastor, which is the content of "De reformatione ecclesiae" in some of its versions; De Frede, pp. 72-3, 78; ASV, Misc. Arm. II 79, fo. 363r, no. 3; Beccadelli, no. 5?; Dudic, no. 6.

DATE:
probably written over a period of at least fifteen years, from the first stirrings of Trent nearly to the end of Pole's life. Many of the versions contain some reference to the need for a council, or to its calling, which provides a *terminus post quem*.

---

[147] Agostino Valier, *Bernardi Navgerii [sic] S. R. E. Cardinalis...Vita*, in Agostino Valier, *De cautione adhibenda in edendis libris* (Padua: Giuseppe Comino, 1719). Gigliola Fragnito, *La Bibbia al rogo: la censura ecclesiastica e i volgarizzamenti della Scrittura (1471-1605)* (Bologna: Il Mulino, 1997), pp. 143, 176-78 and passim.

Catalogue of Works

MSS:
The difficulty of sorting out the numerous versions is heightened by the fact that those in Vat. lat. 5964 are bound in the volume roughly in reverse order of composition. It is impossible to do much codicology, either, because of restoration. Nevertheless, the discovery of the ACDFSO MS, the final version, allows fair confidence in the sequence of texts suggested here. Cf. e.g., the incipit which appears in the top margin of b) and opening definition. Original form: "Reformari quidem ecclesiam intelligimus cum ea ad primae formae pulchritudinem revocatur" entirely cancelled; final version apparently "Reformari quidem ecclesia dicitur cum ad prioris formae pulchritudinem revocatur"), which runs very close to the incipit of b).

a) ACDFSO, St. st. E-6-a, fasc. 2, fos. 1-59. Probably in Dudic's hand, with Binardi's corrections. Six quires, stitched together, numbered at head in Arabic and in lower left in Roman numerals. Foliated in upper right corner. Scriptural tags in margin. Cover page like those in Vat. lat. "Dialogi Card. de reformatione ecclesiastica Quint. VI postremum correti." "No. 26" [*ov.* "26"] at left margin. "27" at top of page. Title page different size paper than text. The incipit of no quire matches Seripando's "Quomodo ergo scripturas interpretari possit populo" (De Frede, p. 73). In.: "Cum ecclesiae reformatio nunc omnibus sit in ore, et ab opt[ime?] quoque iampridem flagitetur: saepe [*ab.* and perhaps autograph] mihi de ea saepe [*del.*] cogitant[em?] potissimum in mentem venerunt, de quibus sententiam tuam sciscitarer, unde scilicet tantum opus ordiri maxime conveniat, et quaenam vera sit eius perficiendi ratio, ac modus, *ut ecclesia recte, atque ordine reformetur [*del.*]. Haec igitur a te nunc explicari cupio: si prius tamen, ut id de quo agitur, plane intelligatur ostenderis [prob. in Binardi's hand *ab. del.* exposueris (orig.) and declaraveris (prob. autograph.)] quid sit ecclesiam reformari." Ex.: "et cognoscere, et exequi possit: ac nisi ita fecerit nullos ei magistros, utcunque doctrina, utcunque vitae sancitate praestantes quicquam esse profituros."

Vat. lat. 5964.1. Volume cover: "De Reformatione Ecclesiae."

A complete collation of fos. 32r-v vs. 72v-73r, 155r-v, 212r-213r, 393v (foot)-394r and 439r-v suggests both the relative independence of versions, and also that Pole worked on "De reformatione" too long, frequently fiddling so much that he accidentally or from memory restored the original text. This raises the question of where the other versions were during later stages of composition. The version at the end of Vat. lat. 5964 may not be the earliest. Cf. fo. 475r: "Summa vero vitae eius haec fuit, ut ab eo tempore, quo eum boni reliquerunt, omnis populus potestas benefaciendi [sic] ei ablata [*ab. del.* "aperta"]," a scribal error which seems to indicate an earlier version yet before this. The versions are listed in reverse order of probable composition, with the most recent first.

a) fos. 52r-84v, and perhaps fos. 85r-134v, which picks up at the same point in text. No heading, nor footer. In Faita's or Dudic's hand, with corrections probably mainly by Binardi. Scriptural tags in margin. Collation: originally foliated 1ff. Fo. 61/11r has "2" and 71/21r "3" in lower left corner. Most folios have tags. This is the latest version in the volume, but it was apparently meant to lead into the same point as c) had reached.[148] It was perhaps intended as the final version, to judge from the scriptural references added in the margin, and the quotation marks, but revisions were made later than both. Whole text covered with brown paper. Total length eighty-one folios. In.: "Cum ecclesiae reformatio nunc in ore, et (?) optime quanquam iam quidem flagitetur: mihi de ea saepe cogitari haec potesse in mentem venerant [*in top mar.*]." Ex.: "meris malis libera id vero est fictae simulationis/ vitium qua vocabulo graeco nostri solent hypocrisia appel/lamus hanc una [picked up as correction from first version, fo. 51v] tollere populo et simul de ecclesia omnia"—tag: quae, which picks up at the top of fo. 85r.

b) fos. 135r -163v? "No. 60" in upper left corner. Fair copy in Faita's or Dudic's hand with autograph corrections. Fo. 135r headed "De reformandae ecclesiae per ministerium [*ab.*] verbi Dei *ad exem-plar eorum qui eadem [*ab. del.* "in formanda"] ecclesiae primi minstri (?) verbi extitere [*del.*]" and foot: "Principium. .

---

[148] Fenlon calls this the "second version" (*Heresy and Obedience*, p. 206).

.fragmen-tum primum De reformatione." Upper left between head and text: "Principium correctum." Collation: only one foliation; most folios have tags; no indications of gatherings. Inc: "Q. Quid est quod dicimus reformari ecclesiam oportere." Ex.: (fo. 162r; cf. fos. 47r-v) "quod ipse populus suas partes, quae sunt maxime in hoc sancto negotio agere negligat, quod nisi agnoscat, nisi confiteatur, nisi veniam supplex pro tanta negligentia a Deo petat frustra quidem cum eo de reformatione agi. si vero fateatur et erroris maximi supplex veniam a patre misericordiarum petat, tum misericordiam consecuturum, tum locum futurum, ut fructuose cum eo de ecclesiae sua reformatione episcopus loqui possit." End original text. Autograph correction follows: "quae principium ducit ab accusatione sui ipsius [*in line of writing* fo. 47v] cum [et] hoc est quod primum in illorum animis plantari et aedificari debet. evulsa tanquam inutili et vitiosa herba ["radice" fo. 47v] omni aliorum accusatione et ["atque ea" fo. 47v] maxime ei [*del.* 47v] quae culpam suorum peccatorum in rectores suos transfert."

c) fos. 314r-323v. In.: "ac deicidas [?= "the fallen"] quantum in se fuit declararunt. Q. An nobis Judae proditoris et Judarum par- ricidarum." Ex.: "quod divitiis hoc modo locupletantur, quas postea in suas cupiditat. His consument (?), vel etiam ut cupidita[sic]." Apparently no tag. Collation: Magiscule "E" [*ab. del.* "D"] lower right corner fo. 314r and possibly magiscule "G" lower left corner. No other pagination/foliation. Perhaps a continuation from either version e) or f)? The substance fits either fos. 130ff or fos. 292ff, but the second is a little nearer the break.

d) BNN, MS IX A. 14, fos. 1r-40v. In (1r): "Saepe mihi cogitanti de ecclesiae reformatione." Fo. 40r blank. Fo. 40v has a few gaps in the first few lines, but could be continued from 39v. Ex.: "ad opera facienda ex lege data habebant. . .descriptione operum sex dierum populum doceri quid sex diebus." In same hand as following letters. Its incipit matches that of f) as emended. This version may have been prepared for the press, judging from the presence in the volume of a copy of Muzzarelli's letter urging Pole to publish.

e) fos. 1br-51v & 85r-134v (but see b) ab.). If these two pieces belong together, the total length is 102 fos. No. 62 centered at head. Fair copy in Faita's hand with autograph corrections.[149] Text at some points apparently independent of apparently earlier versions, e.g., fo. 47r vs. 161v-62r. Resumed fo. 314r (fragment no. 7)? Fo. 1br *disiectum membrum* in Faita's hand. Inc: "Saepe mihi cogitanti [*ab. del.* "cum mihi"] de ecclesiae reformatione cogitanti [*del.*]." Emended version matches incipit of d). Ex.: "quando aut intelligi ecclesiam reformari." Tag of "R." In.: "Q. Quid est, quod dicimus reformari ecclesiam oportere hoc enim modo loquendi utuntur fere omnes qui concilium generale necessarium hiis temporibus esse iudicant," all cancelled and replaced with "R. Reformari quidem vel ecclesiam, vel hominem tum intelligimus [*ab. del.*"dicimus"], cum ad primae formae pulchritudinem vel singuli homines. . . ." Ex. (fo. 51v): "hanc unam tolla populo et simul de ecclesia omnia, quae [tag]" (to fo. 85r). Ex. (fo. 134v): End of R.'s speech beginning on fo. 130r (mostly deleted to end this version). Begins: "Narrant quidem evangelistae sacerdotes populum contra Christum concitasse et multo maior est miseria quae nobis, quod Deus avertat, impendet nisi poenitentia ducti Christi verbo intus loquenti suum honorem reddiderimus. Haec vero sunt quae priori loco episcopus populo auribus, et cordibus assidue instillare, vel potius fulminare, et tonare debet, quibus in terram superba eorum colla pros-ternantur, si eos reformatos esse cupiat, ut intelligere eos faciat fontem deformationis corporis Christi, quod est ecclesia, ab ipsis incipere, quod antequam intelligant, et cum animi dolore agnos-cant, nunquam sane vite reformari possunt." The text ends in the middle of the line, without a tag. Collation: fo. 2r (orig. fo. 1) has magiscule "A" in lower left corner; fo. 12 "B;" fo. 23 "C;" fo. 35 "D;" fo. 85r "E" (with large 4 above it); fo. 95 "F or 5 (?)"; fo. 125 "8." Fo. 1b was added, and the rest of the foliation increased by one through fo. 5. Thereafter there is only one foliation. The original foliation is perhaps in the same hand as the volume title. Fos. 26 and 27 on smaller paper and out of place; fo. 27 stops mid-folio. Tag on fo. 25v ("introirent") matches fo. 28r. Fos. 2-11, 15-25, 28-39, 47-51, 85r-134 all same large, heavy paper. Intervening fos. in smaller, lighter paper.

---

[149] Fenlon labels this the "first draft" (ibid.).

Single foliation to fo. 51, then orig. fos. 1-33 (now fos. 52-84), then fos. 31-80 (now fos. 85-134). In. (fo. 26r): "Cur doctrina quietis (?) eam [ab.] esse dicis, eam [del.] quamvis (?) quo fidem spem et dilectionem nostram." Ex. (fo. 27v): "*Quid tandem dicis esse baptizare verbo patris" [aft. del. "idem est quod dicimus verbo baptizare"]. Fos. 39v-40r dis-continuous. The tag "animi" on fo. 39v is not found in the rest of this version. It probably continues on fo. 47r, despite missing tag. Ex. (fo. 39v): "*quam reformatio quo nomine intelligitur commune omnium ordinum bonum per illos impediatur quod verbis simu-lant se cupere reformationem et factis atque exemplo magis magisque suo eam deforment. Q. Quid vero tu an hoc tanquam iniustam accusationem ex animis [del.]." Fos. 40-46 smaller paper. Text appears to be continuous through fo. 43, picked up on fo. 46. Fo. 44 apparently out of place, but too light to read. Fo. 45 blank. In. (fo. 40r): "docentes servare omnia quaecunque (?) nobis, Haec vero secunda pars mandatorum Christi continens." Ex.: "dico ut ab universo populo intelligi queat, si pastores populorum ut ipsi accusantorum (?)" (one-third page blank). Fo. 47r may pick up from fo. 38v, although it should have an "E" for gathering, which does not appear until fo. 85r. From fo. 51v to 85r (orig-inally fo. 31, but there is such a number in this text already) most folios have tags.

f) fos. 244r-93v. It has no heading nor note at foot, save a magiuscule "A" in the lower right corner and "1" in lower left. There are no other such numbers later. In.: "Q. An tu igitur ita censas in conformando presenti. . . ." Ex.: "R. . . .dum [donec] per sacerdotes rumor est iniectus, si Christum favere pergerent de patria, *de liberate [tag]." Collation: Paginated 1-99 in upper right. Tags between fos. 253-4; 263-4; 273-4; 283-4; 293 does not match 294. Many of the few corrections are in the hand of the copyist, but some are autograph (e.g., fos. 252r, 282v).

g) fos. 294r-313v. Fo. 294r foot: "Fragmentum tertium sequitur de reformatione tractanda (?) pertinebant." In.: "Q. Quid tandem in Danielis oratione, et exemplo pro populo captivus orantis (?) animadverte, quodnam si hoc tempore." Ex. (313v): "hic vero est ille puer de qui propheta Isaias in persona Dei patris scribes dicit. Ecce puer meus quem elegi, di (tag: lectus)." The text may continue in a note on the bottom half of fo. 483r, but there is no textual warrant for making the connection. Fo. 483v top may continue from both notes on fo. 483r. Collation: no other foliation/pagination.

h) fos. 324r-50v. Foot 324r: "Fragmentum quartum" (rest illegible). In.: "et ecclesiae malis providere, et in maiores difficultates ipsi si coniecerunt, et maiorem simul rerum omnium perturbationem in ecclesiam." Ex.: "eo apud hos (?) propheta quae rare in tuo te configuntur (?) quibus respondet propheta in personam Dei in decimis et primitiis et in penuria vos maledictos et me configitis gens tota." Collation: "2" lower right corner, fo. 324r. No other apparent foliation nor pagination. To judge from the hand of the autograph corrections, this is an early version. The text varies a great deal from version f), and the differences support this text's priority, e.g., fos. 105v/268v-269r/336v-337r, where fo. 337r heavily corrected.

i) fos. 164r-243v? Footer: "De reformatione: Fragmentum secundum sine fine." Collation: Only present foliation. Foliation possibly in hand of cover. Fo. 164r has "1" in lower left corner; fo. 174 "2"; fo. 184 "3"; fo. 194 "4"; fo. 204 "5"; fo. 214 "6"; fo. 224 "7"; fo. 234 "8." Tags between fos. 203-204; 213-14; 243v (but succeeding folio not found). In.: "Q. Quid est quod dicimus reformari ecclesiam oportere, hoc enim modo loquendi utuntur fere omnes." Ex.: "Q. An si in Saulis vitae exitu aliqua ostenduntur quae non parvam similitudinem reddunt passionis Christi, eadem in aliorum regum vita [tag: quo]." Cf. ex. of version k). Incomplete. The lack of many corrections suggests that this may be an abandoned version. It diverges radically from later texts at fo. 218v.

j) fos. 351r-410v?. Footer: "Fragmentum quintum de reformatione circa populum." In.: "Q. 1. Quid est quod dicimus reformari ecclesiam oportere, hoc enim modo loquendi utuntur fere omnes qui concilium quidem necessarium hiis temporibus esse iudicant." Ex.: "conversisse (?) si vero spiritui (?) exercio (?) (illegible word) hoc expressit, quod illi qui se reges faciunt, qui fortunatissimi videntur [tag: in sua ult (?)]." Collation: No other apparent foliation nor pagination. Tags are found on fos. 360-361, 380-81, 390-91, 400-01, and 410 (which does not match 411), but not 370-71.

Fo. 361r has "2" in lower left corner; fo. 371 "3"; fo. 381r "4" and "D" lower right corner; 391r "5"/"E"; fo. 401 "F."

k) fos. 411r-443v?, probably resuming on fos. 449r-476v? (half-page blank). No indication of new text. Apparently another version of text on fos. 173r-v/359r-v. Unknown hand. In. (fo. 359v/411r): "propitius esto tibi, quod quidem huiusmodi videtur, qui nullum benevoli serium (?) signum Petrus maius (?) dare Christo potuerit, et ideo laude (?) potius, quam vituperatione dignus (?) videri possit? R. Apud homines quidem laude iam (?) dignum videri potest, quo in Petro (?) verum hoc ipsum est, quod in principe." Ex.: "Q. An si in Saulis vitae exitu aliquo ostenduntur, quae non parvam similitudinem reddunt passionis Christi (?) eadem in aliorum rerum vita [tag: quo]." Cf. ex. of i). Collation: fo. 411 "2" lower left; fo. 421 "3"; fo. 429 "4" (but sequence between gatherings is correct); fo. 439 "5"; fo. 454 "6 (?)" and "X." Tags on fos. 420v; 428v; 438v; 453v; 463v; 475v (which does not match fo. 476r). No other apparent foliation/pagination. "R" and "Q" are often added and the text sometimes has no break between question and response.

l) fo. 444 autograph notes, apparently a draft of fo. 408r; fos. 445r-48v in part apparently a fair copy after the mess of fos. 402r-407v (version j) with autograph text. On the second half of fo. 448r and 448v is a version prior to a passage in i). Fo. 476r-v is an earlier version of fos. 372r/421r. Therefore there may perhaps be two versions of this passage in j)?

m) Perhaps a translation was intended but never completed. Cf. the title in Vat. lat. 5966, fo. 2r: "Dialogus volg. appartanente alla Riforma trattato altrimenti nelli libri dell'off. del Pont."

9) "De officio regis," dialogue with Queen Mary.

ATTESTATIONS: De Frede, pp. 78 (1 February 1556), 80 (Seripando's reply of 31 March asking to see the work), 100 (?), 105 (?).

DATE:
None possible, except vaguely 1553-1558. It may well have been written before Pole returned to England, given its stress on the

problem of the cupidity of the great and Mary's wish for consolation once she had performed true penance.[150] The work was certainly begun by early 1556. The extant version may date from quite late in the reign, to judge from its emphasis on consolation.

MSS:
The two possibilities do not overlap in content and either could be the work referred to by Feria in no. 41 below.

   a) Vat. lat. 5970.2, fos. 369r-74v. Title on fo. 368r: "79 Fragmentum Dialogi habiti cum Maria Regina Manu D. Card." In.: "his quidem mediis usus esse video tam illos quam apostolos ut populum." Ex.: "nisi quos innocens ducentibus (?) est. Sed quid hoc innocentiae proficeret quo (?) (illegible word) me ipsi quod (?)."

   b) ACDFSO, St. st. E-6-a, fasc. 9. Dialogue between "Mar. Reg." i. e., Maria Regina] and "Reg. Car." [Reginaldus Cardinalis]. Octavo. Probably in Faita's hand, with corrections almost certainly in Binardi's, and a few in a very small, unknown hand, but perhaps Faita's (e.g., fo. 85r). Collation: original foliation 81-104, plus one more leaf of another gathering, perhaps in Binardi's hand. Continuous text. Watermark perhaps of fountain. In.: "taverint, et demonia eiecerint, et multaque alia signa fecerint, dicturus est. Nescio vos. Ite maledicti in ignem aeternum." Ex.: "haec si Maestas contrito, et humilitate corde fecerit, dubitare non debet, quin laetitia salutaris Dei ipsi imperitia, principali, vereque regio, et munifico Christi spiritu confirmetur, quae vera, et solida est afflicta ac moerentis [*mar.*] animi [*correction from* animae] consolatio."

10) Sermons.

Six pieces are identified in the manuscripts as sermons, and there is evidence that at least six more (perhaps including a missing item) deserve that designation, for a certain total of at least

---

[150] Mary may have referred to this work in a letter to Pole of 15 November [1553], hoping that "tuis scriptis" would provide her consolation. *CRP*, no. 757.

twelve (or as many as fourteen counting two doubtful pieces in the catalogue), not including the address to the Council of Trent (catalogue no. 36).[151] Beccadelli's identification of n) as a sermon may mean that texts such as catalogue no. 13 deserve that label as well.[152] Together with various other hortatory works perhaps intended for public dissemination (not all included in this catalogue because of doubts about their precise status), the total of sermons might rise as high as twenty.

ATTESTATIONS: De Frede, p. 100; Dudic, no. 18 ("Homilias tres, quae in Latinum sermonem conversae sunt"); Wood, no. 20; Tanner.

DATES:
a-c) were planned as a unit (Vat. lat. 5968, fo. 446r), intended to be printed (fo. 419v). The first can be dated 25 March 1556, the day of Pole's consecration as archbishop of Canterbury in the Canterbury peculiar of St. Mary-Arches, London.[153] The other two present difficulties. There is no internal indication of a possible date for either b) or c), except that they came after a). B) may never have been delivered, but intended only for print. It is in part an attack on Cranmer, which may mean that it came fairly soon after Pole's first sermon in March 1556 and must predate the revocation of his legation in April 1557. That all three were planned as a unit may mean they belong fairly closely together in time. D) and h) were both apparently preached on St. Andrew's Day (30 November), the anniversary of the reconciliation of England.[154] Given the chaos surrounding the calling of the London synod in October and November 1555, it seems unlikely that the series could have begun then. D) probably

---

[151] For discussion of Pole's preaching, see *Prince and Prophet*, chapter 6.

[152] Beccadelli, p. 314.

[153] *CRP*, no. 1524.

[154] Since h's) pericope was probably "Laetatus sum," an unidentified Psalms text, I have assumed that d), which used the same pericope, was preached on the same occasion. I am grateful to Susan Wabuda for help on this point.

postdates Cranmer's execution and probably belongs to 1556.[155] H) seems necessarily to be from 1557, given its reference to the reconciliation which occurred three years ago.[156] The difficulty for this theory is that the diarist Henry Machyn recorded a sermon of 30 November 1557 for the installation of Sir Thomas Tresham, which he did not link to the anniversary of the reconciliation; Strype pronounced it lost [i) *bel.*].[157] H) celebrates the reconciliation and makes no reference to Tresham or the knights of St. John of Jerusalem, but Pole's sense of rhetorical occasion could be notoriously weak. If h) was the sermon delivered for Tresham's installation, then there is no missing sermon of that date, or it may be that he delivered two sermons on 30 November 1557. Pole still meant to publish these sermons in June 1558, at the same time as he claimed that "Since I have often preached in this metropolitan church and many other places in the diocese, then twice in London, nor afterwards, with the help of God's grace, as I hope, will it [a sermon] be lacking" ("Cum enim in ipsa metropolitana ecclesia et nonnullis illis dioecesis meae locis praedicavi saepius, tum etiam Londini bis, neque posthac, juvante Dei gratia, ut spero, deerit").[158] N) was delivered 28 November 1554.

MSS:

Vat. lat. 5968:

a) 1) fos. 379r-99r. Title: "Copia prima Omelia." Scribal draft with corrections. 2) fos. 401r(402r)-18r. Title: "Homilia prima Anglice scripta. No. 100 (?)," fair copy. 3) fo. 34r-v, autograph draft, perhaps continued on fos. 478rff. In.: "Most dearly beloved

---

[155] Pogson, "Cardinal Pole," p. 190 said it dates from perhaps 1557, but on p. 203n, he guessed 1555.

[156] John Strype, *Ecclesiastical Memorials Relating Chiefly to Religion, and its Reformation, under the Reigns of King Henry VIII, King Edward VI, and Queen Mary*, seven volumes (Oxford: Clarendon Press, 1816), 3:2, pp. 498-99 and cf. p. 40.

[157] *The Diary of Henry Machyn*, ed. John Gough Nichols (London: Camden Society, 1848, original series no. 42), p. 159. Strype, *Ecclesiastical Memorials*, 3:2, p. 21.

[158] *CRP*, no. 2252.

in Iesu Christe." Ex.: illegible. Collation: fo. 34r-v, six lines on 43r (rest of fo. blank.), fos. 44r-51r (discussion of peace), then back to fos. 35r-42v, although this could be a separate sermon. Title on fo. 257v upside down and deleted: "Homilie Anglice Prima et secunda Traduttione del Faita della predica di S.to Andrea." According to Faita the sermon was given "all'improviso."[159] Fortunately, this is either not true or Pole sat down very soon afterwards and wrote out his text. Although Faita said he had done a poor job of recording Pole's words, his text runs close to Pole's which must mean that Pole had prepared his remarks in advance or that Faita had Pole's draft before him when he pretended to write his report from his own notes. In any case, there is very little variation between the two main texts.[160]

b) fos. 419r-41r. "Secunda Omelia." In English. On fo. 428r is the highly interesting marginal note "sensus in Anglico sermone non satis constat." Cf. PRO, SP 69/8, no. 490, fos. 94r-112r, fair copy in Italian, in Faita's hand. Dixon claimed that this was the sermon prepared for Pole's installation at Canterbury.[161]

c) fos. 446r-82v. "Homilia Tertia Anglie [sic]" (there were only "Homiliae duae" according to the index of the volume). Scribal copy with corrections, some autograph. Imperfect. Col-lation:

---

[159] *CRP*, no. 1557. Pole's oration to parliament, which also seemed to be given *ex tempore*, was preceded by drafts. John Elder, *Copie of a letter sent into Scotlande* (London: John Wayland, 1555), sigs. Dv and Eiir.

[160] The original Protestant judgment of this sermon proved long-lived. The authors of *De antiquitate britannicae ecclesiae* (London: [John Daye], 1572), Matthew Parker, John Joscelyn and George Acworth described it as "tam exilem & ieiunam orationem...ut non modo de Theologia nihil sapuisse, sed in ipsa, cui diu studuerat oratoris facultate atque copia exaruisse visus est" (p. 418), an assessment that Bishop Burnet borrowed, calling the sermon "cold...without either learning or eloquence...for eloquence, though in his younger days... his style was too luxuriant and florid, yet...he turned as much to the other extreme, and cutting off all ornaments of speech he brought his style to a flatness that had neither life nor beauty in it." Nicholas Pocock, ed., *The History of the Reformation of the Church of England by Gilbert Burnet*, seven volumes (Oxford: Clarendon Press, 1865), 2, p. 545. How either Parker et al. or Burnet knew the sermon is unknown.

[161] Dixon, *Church of England*, 4, p. 559.

Orig. foliation 1-22 to fo. 468r, where 69, 70, 71, 72 added in pencil below new foliation. Perhaps an indication that the collation continued, but the first text ends at the foot of fo. 468v. Fo. 473 *disiectum membrum*. Fos. 474r-77v continuous. Autograph from fo. 478r. Perhaps continued from fo. 42v.

d) fos. 277r-303v, perhaps continued on fos. 227r-47v ("A fragment towchinge the sacrament of the altare") and again on fos. 248r-56v, although this apparent continuity might be a function merely of similar content. Title: "Pars sermonis que cepit laetatus sum, Anglice" ("Homilia .1. super psalmum laetatus sum" according to the index). Cf. the *disiectum membrum* in Vat. lat. 5970, fo. 385v (mounted upside down), "[no.] 37 Homilia del Car.le tradotta dal Faita," which may refer to this sermon.

e) fos. 35r-42v. Probably a sermon on virginity.

f) fos. ?16r-17r, perhaps continued on fos. 18r-21r. Title: "super die veneris sancto Apon good fridaye." Autograph draft in English.

g) fos. ?22r-23r. Title: "Super eo Quia audisti me Thoma credidisti Beati." Autograph draft. This could as well be a scripture commentary.

h) a fragment in Strype, *Eccl. Mem.*, 3:2, pp. 482-510, misleadingly titled "Cardinal Pole's speech to the citizens of London, in behalf of religious houses."

MS: none. It was said to be from "Foxii MSS," so if it survives it should be in the BL, Inner Temple Library, or Emmanuel College Library, but it has not been found. According to a private communication from Thomas Freeman, there have been losses from Foxe's papers, mainly when they were in Strype's possession.

i) Machyn's sermon on Tresham's installation 30 November 1557, although this may really be h).

j) Vat. lat. 5968, fos. 1ar-4v, headed "Ad sacerdotes in synodo." The text is in English. Pogson and J. P. Marmion identify it as the opening sermon, but its reference to the model of the archdeacon's annual report in "this holy tyme of Lent" to be followed by the bishops returning to their dioceses must mean

that it was read in February 1556.[162]
EDITIONS: Brassell (1935), app. 3, pp. 322-35; Marmion, 2, pp. 81-93 (from Brassel).

k) fo. 8r-v. Headed "Ad sacerdotes in synodo." Autograph draft. On fos. 10-12r is a list of "Quaenam cum episcopis tracatanda erunt." This may appear to contain some of Pole's agenda, if for no other reason than its reference to *hoc synodo* (fo. 10r). If so, it would have to date from early on in it, since it refers to Gardiner as present and he died on 12 November. The fact that it is addressed solely to the bishops does not make against the possibility of a connection to the synod, since Pole seems to have viewed them as far its most important constituent. There are, however, at least three main reasons for discounting *hoc synodo*. First, the document is one of a number of similar texts directed to the bishops, most of which have no obvious links to the synod.[163] Second, the document is entirely concerned with the provision of good bishops, and about half of it details how their status was to be or had been regularized. Third and most important, once the matter of the bishops' status was dealt with, Pole proceeded to give instructions for how they were to reconcile their dioceses. Both the provision of bishops, including the example of Edmund Bonner given in the memo, and the reconciliation had been largely taken care of by February 1555. This makes it appear more likely that the text reflected Pole's plans in the immediate aftermath of his return to England, which included a synod, than those for its meeting in December.
EDITIONS:
Brassell (1935), pp. 336-9; Marmion, 2, pp. 94-99.

l) fos. 6r-7v. Headed "Super illi imitatores mei estatis (?)." Autograph draft. This may be a text related to the last two.

m) Vat. lat. 5966, fos. 41r probably to 44v, autograph draft.

---

[162] Pogson, "Cardinal Pole," p. 164. J. P. Marmion, "The London Synod of Reginald, Cardinal Pole, 1555-6," two volumes (Keele University M. A. thesis, 1974), 2, pp. 76-78.

[163] For the prominence of the bishops in Pole's thinking about the synod, see, e.g., *CRP*, no. 1414 or De Frede, p. 76.

Date: The incipit of a letter in English on fo. 39v may help a little to date this sheaf of documents. It is addressed to "the datary of the pope," apparently meaning Cardinal Scotti, and replies to his letter brought by Goldwell, who returned to England by 15 December 1555. This was perhaps a draft of Pole's opening remarks to the London synod.

   n) Versions in Italian or Latin
1) ASV, Segreteria di Stato, Inghilterra 3, fos. 156r-8v, probably in Faita's hand;
2) ASV, Nunz. div. 145, fos. 143r-49r (copy);
3) included in the summary of proceedings in parliament in Folger Shakespeare Library, W. b. 132 (78) (Strozzi transcripts), fos. 111r-16v;
4) ASV, Fondo Carpegna 202, fos. 98r-101v;
5) BL, Add. MS 15388, fos. 311-19;
6) Cambridge University Library, Add. MS 4832 (copy for Lord Acton of PBN, Fond ital. 1281), fos. 128-33;
7) ASV, Fondo Borghese II, 483 B, fos. 124r-28v; cf. Latin version in ASV, Fondo Borghese I, 976, fo. 17.
Versions in English
1) Vat. lat. 5968, fos 305r-59r, headed "Ad concilium parliamenti." Scribal copy (reading text?). Original foliation 1-55;
2) fos 129r-45v, autograph draft;
3) fos 361r-76v, no. 4, "Ad consilium parlamenti," another draft with some autograph corrections.

11) "De modo concionandi."

ATTESTATIONS AND DATE: *CRP*, no. 345, Pole asking Cardinal Contarini's help with his work on preaching and reporting a preacher's reactions, perhaps Nicolás Bobadilla's; ASV, Misc. Arm. II 79, fo. 363r, no. 1; Beccadelli, no. 4; Dudic, no. 7; *Proc. Carn.*, p. 447; *PM*, 1, p. 198 (the only work listed in the compendium of charges against Pole); *PM*, 6, p. 174 (Bernardo de' Bartoli's first deposition, saying that Vittoria Colonna had a copy and p. 177 admitting that he knew of the work); no such, according to William Lyde;[164] Wood, no. 18 ("'Tis a large volume, but imperfect"); Dodd, no. 17 ("Volumen de modo concionandi. Opus imperfectum. MS."); Tanner; Cooper, who lists it among MSS at Douai.

MS: none known. The only trace of it may be the single sheet in Vat. lat. 5968, fo. 444r headed "We thinck yt were good that yt were more at large proved bothe by scripture, ensample and authoryte of the fathers that everye man sholde not be his owne teacher by reading alone scripture," although this could also serve as a summary of the previous sermon. The text printed in *ERP*, 3, pp. 75ff is not Pole's; cf. *PM*, 6, p. 174n.

Given that this is one of only a few of Pole's alleged works to have disappeared without a trace, it seems likely that it must be hiding behind the title of some other work.

12) "De officio Romani Pontificis et de eius electione" (*De summo pontifice*).

ATTESTATIONS: ASV, Misc. Arm. II 79, fo. 363r, no. 2; *Proc. Carn.*, p. 447; *CRP*, no. 1023; Beccadelli, no. 3; Dudic, nos. 4 and 5; Possevino; *Nomenclator*; Torrigio; Ghilini; Freher; Wood, no. 10, including the five books *extra conclavi*; Dodd, no. 10 (Louvain, 1569); Tanner (Louvain, 1569); Cooper.

DATE:
begun in the conclave of Julius III, and continued thereafter, perhaps only until Pole left Rome in May 1553.

MSS:
of printed text (*intra conclavi*):

a) Douai, Bibliothèque municipale, MS 922, 4, pp. 1-89, dedication letter and fair copy. Unknown hand, but perhaps Pyning's. The incipit and explicit match the printed edition. It was in the English College, Douai as of 1748 (BCQ, MS F. III. 7

---

[164] *Some observations upon the life of Reginaldus Polus Cardinal....* (London: Matthew Turner, 1686), p. 59.

m. 1, fo. 49r), when listed as a separate item from Pole's legatine register. Tootell did not mention it thirty years earlier, despite including the larger set of MSS which contains it in his bibliography.

b) ACDFSO, St. st. E- 6-a, fasc. 5, foliated. Includes dedication to della Rovere. Fair copy in Faita's or Dudic's hand, with corrections, some probably in Priuli's hand. Scriptural tags in margin. Seventy-six numbered folios, plus four blank at end. In.: "Urb. Cum mihi hesterno tuo sermone satis esset persuasum in eo negotio." Ex.: "Urb. Ita faciam eique nunc [*ab. del.* atque] vivm, quod in tanta re hoc tempore talem mihi hypodidascalum dederit." Note at foot: "Imprimatur sed a S. D. N. R.mo Vic. prius videretur: Frater Petrus Paulus Giannarinus de Arrectio Magister Sacri Palatii [new line] Vir. (?)."

Vat. lat. 5972:

c) fos. 1r-77r. Corrected. Includes dedication.

d) fos. 79rff. Not identical to print, no dedication. Heavily corrected at the beginning. Imperfect.

e) fos. 139r-169b, continued on fos. 170r-87v. With dedication, almost identical with print. Incomplete?

f) fos. 192r-285r. Without dedication. Close to print. Corrections. At least two versions.

g) Vat. lat. 5966, fos. 133r-201v. Italian. In.: "A che modo deve portarsi il sommo pastore." Ex.: "che Dio tenne nel formarlo non. . . .tempio tra la parola [tag]." From fo. 201v would appear to become *extra conclavi*. Brown paper. Fair copy, probably in two hands, with corrections in Pole's hand and possibly one other. Collation: originally a separate work, foliated 1ff. Interlocutors: Urb. Pri. Polus. The relationship between the Italian and Latin versions has not been worked out.

EDITION:

a) De summo pontifice (Louvain: John Fowler, 1569). According to the preface to Pius V by Henry Jolliffe, English priest, it came from a manuscript Pyning had. From 1555-59 the printer Fowler (born 1537) was a Fellow of New College along with Nicholas Sander and John Rastell. In 1565 he was admitted as a stationer of Louvain, which he remained until 1577 (or perhaps 1575).[165] He published thirty-one controversial and devotional works in English.[166] Joliffe was a graduate of Cambridge, and canon of Worcester, including during Richard Pate's tenure as bishop, and had been a witness against Cranmer, as well as dean of Bristol under Mary. He fled to Louvain in 1559 and at some point tried to make a claim against Pate's will. He died 10 August 1573.[167] b) Rocaberti, pp. 141-90. Despite Pole's promise to Truchsess to publish the work in Dillingen, Mayer's press never issued a version (cf. p. 25 ab.).

h) An independent version? Vat. lat. 5965.1, fos. 129r-216v and 5965.2 to end? "De officio papae scripta in conclavi." Autograph? It does not appear to be equivalent to the earlier versions in this volume. Brown paper, barely legible.

of *extra conclavi*:

ATTESTATION: *PM*, 6, pp. 273-4n (Apollonio Merenda's confession). Italian orig.:

i) ACDFSO, St. st. E-6-a, fasc. 4. All five books, nearly complete. This is almost certainly the version referred to by Mer-

---

[165] T. H. Aston, ed., *The History of the University of Oxford*, 3, ed. J. K. McConica, *The Collegiate University* (Oxford: Oxford University Press, 1986), p. 386.

[166] A. C. Southern, *Elizabethan Recusant Prose 1559-1582* (London: Sands and Co., 1950), pp. 338-9 and 342. For Fowler, see also Rouzet, *Dictionnaire*, pp. 64-65, which does not, however, mention Pole's work and differs from Southern's account mainly in claiming that Fowler was also a printer, not merely a publisher.

[167] Gillow, *Biographical Dictionary*, 3, pp. 646-47; "Processus contra Thomam Cranmer" in John Strype, *Memorials of the Most Reverend Father in God Thomas Cranmer*, ed. Philip Edward Barnes, two volumes (London: George Routledge, 1853), 2, p. 499; and J. H. Pollen, ed., 'Dr Nicholas Sander's report to Cardinal Moroni', *Catholic Record Society*, 1 (1905): pp. 1-47, p. 23 *(Calendar of State Papers...Rome, 1, 1558-1571*, ed. J. M. Rigg [London: HMSO, 1916], p. 70). William Maziere Brady, *The episcopal succession in England, Scotland and Ireland A.D. 1400 to 1875*, with a new intro. by A. F. Allison [No place]: Gregg Press, 1971), 2, p. 289; and Christian Coppens, *Reading in Exile: the Libraries of John Ramridge (d. 1568), Thomas Harding (d. 1572) and Henry Joliffe (d. 1573), Recusants in Louvain* (Scottsdale, AZ: L P Publications, 1993), pp. 213-26 for his will and p. 226 for the date of his death.

enda, although part of the version in Vat. lat. 5966 is also possible. Fair copy, probably in Faita's hand, with corrections by same hand as on fasc. 3, and others in Priuli's hand. Divided into four (?) books. Characters identified in the margin in pencil, along with scriptural tags. Book 1 twenty-eight folios (28r-v mostly blank). In.: "Urb. Io hebbi experientia del paterno vostro amore verso di me mentre eravamo in conclavi." Ex.: "Urb. Et cosi Dio per sua bonta mi doni gratia di fare." Book 2 thirty-four folios. In.: "Urb. Io torno a voi Mon. mio per chiedervi la satisfat-tione della promessa che mi feste [sic] hieri." Ex.: "la bonta divina si habbia a communicare della sua gratia nell'avenire, quanto noi saremo piu pronti a ringratiarlo di quella, che egli ci ha infino ad hora concesso." Book 5 follows, without identification, because the first leaf is missing. Next fol. 2 and text not continuous. Twenty numbered folios. In.: (after six lines deleted) "Urb. Veramente ho conosciuto per prova che vi sono assai piu suiamenti (?) che io non havera mai pensato." Ex.: "Ma un'altra gratia di piu desidero et la prego sia contenta farmi, cio e di ricordarsi spesso di me." Incomplete, but probably only a few lines on the last folio are missing. Bk 3, "A" at lower left, unfoliated. In.: "Quanto piu vo pensando sopra il dubbio, che voi Mon. di Urbino hieri proponeste" [11r] "B" in lower left. Total of twenty-four unfoliated folios, then 25 (only numbered folio), "C" in lower left, followed by fourteen folios (most of 14r-v blank). Ex.: "Urb. A me sara sommamente grato d'essere instrutto et udir il poner uno in questa si necessaria, et utile materia, et mi pare benissimo rimettere questo ragionamento a dimani." Bk 4. "A" lower left. Unfoliated. In.: "Pol. Poi che io vi vedo desideroso di intendere il parer mio nelle dimande fatte hieri che da voi Ms. aloisi." Note at foot fo. 23r: "Questi dui capi da le sacrae scripturis (?) et da (?) le (?) ceremoniis accurantia (?) sunt considerandum." Thirty folios, followed by one blank. Ex.: "all'officio suo havendo proposito di essequirle puo esser certo, che la speranza sua non lo ingannera mai."

j) BNM, Ms. Lat. IV, 114 (2304), fo. 172r. "Dell'officio del sommo Pontifice lib. 5 [*ov.* 4] scritti fuori di conclavi No. 37 [*aft. del.* "18"]. Copia piu corretta. il primo libro è in mano di ms. Alvigi Contarino. il 2.o anchora s'è dato al medesimo." Perhaps in the hand of the title on Vat. lat. 5969, fo. 314r (Morone's?). This must refer to a different text than that in ACDFSO.

Catalogue of Works

Latin translations:

According to Merenda, della Rovere translated the *extra conclavi* version into Latin (*PM*, 6, p. 274n.) One of these may be his work.

Vat. lat. 5965.1:

k) fos. 1r-23r. "Extra conclavi scripta de officio pontificis. Prima [*ab. del.* "84"] Pars dialogum (?) de off. pont. extra [*aft. del.* "fuit a scrips"] conclavi scriptum ex Italo sermone in latinum conversa." Book 1 only.

l) fos. 24r-80r. "Pars dialogi de officio pontificis." Book 1 only.

m) fos. 81r-107v. "Liber quintus Dialogorum de officio papae ex conclave scriptorum ex italica lingua in latinam convertus No. 43 ["109" *del.*] Duplic."

n) fos. 108r-28v. Another copy of book 5.

o) ACDFSO, St. st. E-6-a, fasc. 7. "Reginaldi Poli cardinalis de pontificis max. officio." Unknown hand, but probably later than the others, and smaller paper than Italian version above. Unfoliated. Most nearly complete translation. The incipit is not identical to that in Vat. lat. 5965, fo. 1br, although it has more or less the same sense, as does the text checked. It must be an independent translation. Collation: Book 1 thirty-two folios. In.: "Urb. Qui tuus erga me amor sit, quem vere paternum appellare possum." Ex.: "Urb. Hoc Deus pro sua benignitate mihi largiatur." Book 2 forty-eight folios. In.: "Urb. Redeo ad te mi Pole, ut quod heri pollicitus es," which is identical to the incipit of fasc. 4. Ex.: "Pol. Haec profecto ratione est confidendum, Deum eo uberius de eius gratia nobis esse impartiturum (?), quo de ea, quam hactenus accepimus, promptius ei gratias egerimus." Book 3, fifty-one folios. In.: "Pol. Quo diligentia optime Urbinas difficul- tatem quam heri proposuisti, mente meum ipse repeto," identical to the incipit of book 3 of the Italian version above, as is the explicit. Ex.: "Urb. . . .sententiam tuam audire, atque in ea erud-iori disputationemque id tam in proximum diem differre commodissimum futurum existimo." Book 4, forty-seven folios. In.: "Pol. Quoniam Vos (?) vehementer cepere animadverto, ut quid nam de quaestionibus his, de quibus tu optime Aloysi heri es percontatus." Ex.: "Pol. pro certo debit habere, nunquam eius spem illum esse fallituram." One blank fol. Book 5, twenty folios. In.: "Urb. Quid a te expectem etiam me tacente optime Pole facile potes intelligere." Ex.: "qui huic muneri sit preficiendus; quod denique nihil aliud est, nisi summus quidam supra omnes."

13) "Sopra la Rosa et la Spada et il Capello."

ATTESTATIONS: ASV, Misc. Arm. II 79, fo. 363r, no. 9; no. 56, "Littera reverendissimi cardinalis Poli de rosa ad regem Angliae," of "Inventario delle scritture che si ricercano dalli signori reverendissimi deputati dal reverendissimo cardinal Morono che fanno alla causa."[168]

DATE:
There is a little obscurity about this. According to a), the ceremony took place after Julius III's death (24 March 1555), the news of which reached England by 6 April at the latest.[169] The Venetian ambassador reported that the nuncio carrying the pope's gifts, Antonio Agustín, had presented them on 26 March, three days after his arrival, but Pole dated the presentation the 28th.[170] The resolution seems to be that Pole was prevented by illness from performing the complete ceremony on the first occasion (whether on the 26th or 28th March), although he did appear in episcopal vestments, Julius having dispensed him for the occasion, and offered prayers.[171] The first date would have very nearly coincided with the proper time for the ceremony as performed by the pope on the fourth Sunday of Lent, 24 March in 1555. Lutz guessed this text dates from April.[172]

MSS:
    Vat. lat. 5968
        a) fos. 183r-86r, "A declaration to the king & the Quene whatt

---

[168] *PM*, 6, p. 404. The editors leave the work unidentified, except for a reference to ASV, Misc. Arm. II 79.

[169] It was sent by Muzzarelli, the nuncio in Brussels, and Pole replied to Philip's letter incorporating the news between 6 and 8 April (the letter is variously dated; see *CRP*, no. 1170). Lutz, *Nuntiaturberichte*, 14, p. 239n2.

[170] *CSPV*, 6:1, no. 37 and *CRP*, no. 1152.

[171] *CRP*, no. 1038.

[172] Lutz, p. 243n10.

ys signifyed by the sword gyrdle and cappe that the pope sent unto them and of the golden rose the fyrst copye." Fair copy in Italic with autograph corrections.

b) fos. 179r(180r)-82r. "The seconde copye of the declaration of the signification of the sword the cappe the gyrdle & golden rose that the pope sent to the kinge & quene of ynglond."

c) Vat. lat. 5967, fos. 344r-45v draft in Faita's hand with corrections in Binardi's hand, in Latin, and almost identical for content to the last.

d) Vat. lat. 5827, fos. 49v-53r (copy of c).

e) BNM, Lat. XI. 60 (6527), fos. 229r-30v (copy of c).

f) Vat. lat. 8430, fos. 184r-87v (eighteenth-century copy of c).

EDITIONS: *ERP*, 5:16, treated as letter; *CSPV*, 6:1, no. 66, dated ?28 April 1555 (summary); *CRP*, no. 1197 (summary).

g) ASAS, 40/112, a series of preparatory writings.
1) a half-page draft of Pole's remarks at the handing over of the rose (with stage directions);
2) another version, one folio long, headed "Benedictio Rosae in quarta Domenica Quadragesimae;"
3) "De Rosa in Domenica, viz quadragesime benedictione et donanda," headed above "Ex rationali divinorum officiorum," one folio long;
4) a sheet of precise directions for Agustín's reception, etc., perhaps with corrections in Binardi's hand;
5) "De Rosa Regina Angliae praesentanda per R.mum Polum Diaconum Car.lem legatum Informatio Magistri Cerem. missa in Angliam ultima Jan. 1555," probably in Binardi's hand. A more carefully written version of 4), including an extra sheet revising the directions for the moment of presentation, perhaps in Binardi's hand.

h) "De ense in nocte Nativitatis Domini dando et benedicendo." Note at head: "Incerte authore," perhaps in Binardi's hand. The final loose sheet in this bundle concerns the history and collection of Peter's pence in England, drawn from Polydore Vergil, and thus may be connected to Ormanetto, who held that office.

14) Instruction to Paul III.

ATTESTATION: none.

DATE:
late 1536 or very early 1537. It concerned plans for a legation to assist the Pilgrimage of Grace.

MSS:
    a) ASV, Misc. Arm. II 11, fos. 429r-38r.
    b) Vat. lat. 13452, fos. 204v-9r, probably an eighteenth-century copy and probably transferred from ASV.
    c) BAV, Urb. lat. 865, fos. 331-9.
    d) BAV, Ottob. 1111, fos. 158-63r, "Instructio super rebus Anglicanis."
    e) BAV, Chigi. lat. Q I. 13. 1 (3004), fos. 1-10, "Informatione sopra le cose d'Inghilterra data dal Cardinal Polo a Papa Paolo 3.o quando vi fu destinato Legato" (seventeenth- or eighteenth-century copy?).
    f) Vat. lat. 7160, fos. 136ff.
    g) Biblioteca Magliabechiana, perhaps cod. VII, Class XXXII according to BCQ, MS F.III.7 m. 1, fo. 44r, notes on Pole's works in the Maglibechiana, perhaps now in the Fondo Magliabechiano of the Biblioteca nazionale centrale, Florence.

EDITIONS:
ERP, 2, pp. cclxxiv-cclxxix (from unknown MS, but perhaps Vat. lat. 7160); *L&P*, 12:2, no. 368 (summary); *CRP*, no. 150 (summary).

15) Instruction for Pole as legate to Charles V.

Attestation and edition in *ERP*, 2, pp. cclxxix-xxx, said to be from MSS.

DATE: 1539.

MSS: none known, although this may be the work once in the Magliabechiana, referred to in the last entry.

16) *De concilio*.

ATTESTATIONS: *Proc. Carn.*, pp. 434, 484-5; Beccadelli, no. 2; Dudic, no. 3; Possevino; *Nomenclator*; Torrigio; Ghilini; Wood, no. 8 (Rome, 1562; Louvain, 1567, 1569, giving Bodleian shelf marks for the editions of 1567 and Philippe Labbé, *Tridentinii concilii Acta et Decreta* [Louvain: Pierre Thielt, 1667]); Dodd, no. 8, citing the same sources, except the spurious 1569 ed.; Tanner, called *De concilio Tridentino* (Venice: Manuzio, 1562; Rome, 1562; Dillingen, 1562; Louvain, 1567 and 1569); Cooper; Zimmermann (Mayer's edition, which Zimmermann may have located); Klaiber, no. 2580.

DATE:

apparently drafted in March and April 1545.[173] There is no certain evidence for that date. According to the preface, Pole had asked Pope Paul to grant him a month free from all other responsibilities in order to reflect on the council before taking up his post as legate in May 1546. That the other legates never noticed this assignment, despite the fact that *De concilio* is either prefaced by or is entirely a letter to them, and that no one else said anything certainly about *De concilio* at this time, raise some doubts about Pole's allegation. Seripando later claimed to have read the work twice, first "at the same time it was written," but he did not say when that was.[174] There are several quasi-mysterious references to Pole's works and plans to publish them which may point to *De concilio*. The first is to a book Pole sent Gonzaga

---

[173] Fenlon, *Heresy and Obedience*, p. 102n takes the preface at face value, as does Herman Josef Sieben, "Eine 'ökumenische' Auslegung von Apg 15 in der Reformationszeit," *Theologie und Philosophie*, 60 (1985), pp. 16-42, pp. 18 and 34.

[174] Hubert Jedin, *Girolamo Seripando. Sein Leben und Denken im Geisteskampf des 16. Jahrhunderts*, two volumes (Würzburg: Augustinus-Verlag, 1984; reprint of Würzburg, 1937 ed.), 2, p. 636.

in June 1545 which may have been *De concilio*.[175] The second, a draft letter to Vittoria Colonna of 12 February 1546 perhaps from Bernardino Maffei, asked her to intercede with Pole to prevent him from publishing "his works" (originally "exhortations"), but the date and the original phrasing suggest rather his opening sermon to the council than *De concilio*, if Maffei was referring to Pole's work and not Priuli's.[176]

MS:

a) BNN, MS VII C. 46, fos. 19r-79v. In unknown hand, with marginal headings. It probably came from Seripando. Fair copy complete with marginal headings intended for the printer, but it is not the prooftext from which Manuzio worked. His book and the manuscript each have both additions and subtractions relative to the other.

b) A lost codex, described in Apostolo Zeno's index of "Epistolae Cardinalis Reginaldi Poli" in "Codex Ms in fol. in Bibliotecha Jacobi Superanci, Patricii et Senatoris Venete. Spectabat (?) ad Ludovico Beccatellum, Archiep. Ragusinum." (BCQ, MS F. III. 7 m. 1, fos. 7r-8r), as ending with "eiusdem Card. Poli liber de concilio." Neither of the closely related MSS (Vat. lat. 5827 and BNM, Lat. XI. 60 [6527], fos. 211r-305r) contain the work, and neither shows any obvious signs of dismemberment.

EDITIONS CHECKED:

De concilio. De baptismo Constantini. Reformatio Angliae ex decretis eiusdem (Rome: Manuzio, 1562; reprint Farnborough, Hants.: Gregg Press, 1962); Dillingen: Sebald Meyer, 1562; Rocaberti, pp. 312-45; Mansi, 33, cc. 941-1003 (from Labbé); Louvain: Pierre Zangre de Thielt, 1567.[177]

17) ***Discorso di pace.***

ATTESTATIONS: Dudic, no. 10; *Nomenclator* (coupled with oration

---

[175] *CRP*, no. 436.

[176] *PM*, 2, p. 707n.

[177] Simoncelli, *Caso*, p. 216.

Catalogue of Works

to Council); Torrigio; Ghilini; Freher; Wood, no. 7; Dodd, no. 6; Tanner (Venice, 1568); Cooper; Klaiber, no. 2571.

DATE:
March 1554. PBN, MS Fran. 3947, fo. 511rff, a French translation of the dedicatory letter, dated 6 April. Fiordibello brought it to Brussels on 14 April and gave the work to Muzzarelli for presentation to Cardinal Granvelle.[178]

MSS:
To those listed in Lutz, *Friedenslegation*, p. 382 should be added:
 a) Vat. lat. 5256, fos. 96r-118v (with both cover letters to Henry II and Charles V).
 b) Vat. lat. 5968, fos. 147r-66r, "A copye of a letter to the french kyng," but including *Di pace*. Draft in English in Secretary hand. Collation: fos. 147r-153r in upper left corner lettered "A-G;" fos. 160r-161r "H-I;" fo. 162r "K;" fo. 166r *disiectum membrum*, to be put after fo. 159v, as indicated by cross at foot fo. 166r and top margin fo. 160r, which seems to mean that the disordering must have happened while the work was still in draft.
EDITION:
Thomas F. Mayer, ed., "An English Version of Cardinal Pole's Appeal for Peace," *Manuscripta*, forthcoming.
 c) PBN, MS Fran. 3947, fo. 511, to Charles V, Melun, 6 April 1554 (cover letter).
 d) PBN, MS Fran. 17294, fos. 201ff. "Harangue à l'empereur," Melun, 5 April.
 e) Marburg, Politisches Archiv des Landgrafen Philipp des Grossmütigen von Hesse, no. 2418, according to *Politisches Archiv des Landgrafen Philpp des Grossmütigen von Hesse. Inventar der Bestände*, ed. Friedrich Küch and Walter Heinemeyer (Osnabrück: O. Zeller, 1965; Marburg: N. G. Elwert, 1954-1959. Publikationen aus den Königlichen preussischen Staatsarchiven, 78, 85; Die historische Kommission für Hessen und Waldeck, Veröffent-lichungen, 24, 1-2), 3, p. 48. I have been unable to confirm this copy.

---
[178] Lutz, *Nuntiaturberichte*, 14, p. 43.

f) An apparently lost MS, noted in the eighteenth-century catalogue of Jacopo Soranzo's library as in codex CCLII. BNM, Ital. X. 139 (6570).

EDITIONS:

a) Discorso di pace di Mons. Reginaldo Polo Cardinale Legato a Carlo V. Imperatore et Henrico II. Re di Francia (s. l., s. d. [1554; possibly two editions of this year];

b) Venice: Nell'Accademia Veneta, 1558; c) Milan: G. A. degli Antonii, 1560; d) Francesco Sansovino, *Delle Orationi volgarmente scritte da diversi huomini* (Venice:1562,1567 [according to the BL catalogue], 1569, 1575); e) Lutz, pp. 381-403; f) trans. into Latin by Jacopo Pholio (Rome: Blado, 1555); reprinted in *ERP*, 4, pp. 403-27.

18) *Testamentum vere christianum, pium ac prudentissimum reverendissimi et illustriss. D. Domini Reginaldi tt. S. Mariae in Cosmedin, S. R. E. Presbyteri Cardinalis, Archiepiscopis Cantuariensis, totius Angliae primatis et apostolicae sedis legati.*

ATTESTATION: *Proc. Carn.*, e.g., p. 277; Klaiber, no. 2579.

DATE:
4 October, proved 8 December 1558 (see below).

The widely-known (and copied) version of 4 October 1558 did not reflect Pole's final wishes, and despite all Priuli's efforts, Pole did not make them known in time to get them written up in proper form.[179] There are no individual bequests recorded in the main will, but to judge from Priuli's difficulties getting Pole's estate settled and his bequests paid, there may have been a separate schedule of individual legacies, although it could as well be that Priuli acted solely at his own discretion.[180]

MSS:
a) PRO, SP 11/14, no. 1.

---

[179] See Priuli's dramatic account in *CRP*, nos 2311 and 2312.

[180] I attempt to reconstruct them in *CRP*, no. 2286.

b) PRO, PROB 11/42A, fos. 107-8.

c) BL, Egerton 1090, fos. 276r-79r.

d) Surrey Record Office, Loseley MS 2011/84, contemporary copy formerly in the collection of W. M. Molyneux of Loseley Park, Guildford, Surrey, inherited from official papers collected by either Sir Thomas Cawarden or Sir William More.[181]

e) BAV, Urb. lat. 819.2, fos. 440r-48v.

f) Biblioteca Ambrosiana, Milan, MS S 98 Sup., fos. 220r-22r.

g) Madrid, Biblioteca nacional, MS 6149 (R5), among some of the records of the *processo* against Carranza, which I have not been able to see.[182] This may be the authentic copy forwarded to Pole's agent Juan Ugalde by Priuli in order to help with the settlement of Pole's estate.[183]

h) other such copies forwarded by Priuli to his brother Antonio in Venice and Antonio Giberti in Rome on 27 November 1558 (*CRP*, nos. 2311-12) have not been found, nor has that sent to Beccadelli which probably included only the preamble.[184]

i) PRO, PROB 10/38. This reference, given in *CSPDom rev.*, is incorrect.[185]

EDITIONS:

a) Dillingen: S. Mayer, 1559;

b) Rome, 1559, referred to in *ERP*, 5, p. 187 and Fabiano E. Bruskewitz, *The Theology of Justification of Reginald Cardinal Pole* (Rome: Patrizio Graziani, 1969; Pontificia universitas Gregoriana, Rome, thesis ad lauream), bibliography, perhaps drawing on *ERP*;

---

[181] *Historical Manuscripts Commission 7th Report Appendix* (London: HMSO, 1879), p. 597. My thanks to Dr. S. G. Roberts, National Register of Archives, for its current location. For More's broad-gauge collecting, see Jennifer Loach, *Parliament and the Crown in the Reign of Mary Tudor* (Oxford: Clarendon Press, 1986), pp. 214-15.

[182] P. O. Kristeller, *Iter italicum, a Finding List of Uncatalogued or Incompletely Catalogued Manuscripts of the Renaissance in Italian and Other Libraries*, six volumes (Leiden and London: E. J. Brill, 1963-1991), 4, p. 529.

[183] *CRP*, no. 2314.

[184] *PM*, 5, p. 420.

[185] I am grateful to Charles Knighton for trying to unravel the origin of this mistaken citation.

c) Riva di Trento, 1562, without publisher, privilege or colophon;[186]

d) partially printed in Chacón, col. 637;

e) *ERP*, 5, pp. 181-87 from the Ambrosiana (with note at the end "In Edito an. MDLIX absque loco impressionis subscribunt quotquot sequuntur," followed by the signatures of Pole and the witnesses);

f) brief abstract printed in Thomas Phillips, *The History of the Life of Reginald Pole*, two volumes (Oxford: William Jackson, 1764), 2, pp. 210-11 (as if from the Ambrosiana, but really from *ERP*);

g) *Wills from Doctors' Commons. A Selection from the Wills of Eminent Persons Proved in the Prerogative Court of Canterbury, 1496-1695*, ed. J. G. Nichols and J. Bruce (Camden Society, old ser., 83 [1863]), pp. 48-53, with further notations "Proved coram domino, at 'Lambhieth' the 8th day of December, 1558, by the oath of Dominus Aloisius Priulus, etc." and "In the margin—Ult. Decembr. 1569. A commission of administration to Lady Katherine Countess of Huntingdon dowager widow, next of kin to the said Archbishop;"

h) according to Strype (*Ecclesiastical Memorials*, 3:2, p. 143), there is a copy in Raphael Holinshead's *Chronicles*, p. 1161, but I have found none in any edition;

i) *CRP*, no. 2286, critical edition.

TRANSLATION: *CSPDom rev.*, no. 824.

19) *Reformatio Angliae*.

ATTESTATIONS: Possevino; *Nomenclator*; Torrigio; Ghilini; Freher; Wood, no. 7 (editions of Rome, 1562 and 1569); Dodd, no. 7 (editions of Rome, 1556 and 1562; Louvain 1569); Tanner (editions of Rome, 1562; Louvain 1569; Venice, 1562); Cooper; Klaiber, no. 2580; Beccadelli-Gheri, Trent, 24 November 1561.[187]

---

[186] For the press at Riva which worked for the Council of Trent, see Hubert Jedin, *Der Quellenapparat der Konzilsgeschichte Pallavicinos* (Rome: SALER, 1940; Miscellanea Historiae Pontificia, 4, no. 6), p. 72.

[187] Fragnito, "Censura," pp. 24n-25.

Catalogue of Works

DATE:
The synod began on 2 December 1555, and the acts were dispatched to Rome on 14 April 1556.[188]

MSS:
a) CCCC, MS 121, no. 11, pp. 7-31.

b) BL, Cotton Cleop. F. 2, fos. 72r-90r, both drafts in an unknown secretary's hand. This is a fair copy, much of it written out as parliamentary legislation often was in the middle of the page, with a few corrections (e.g., fo. 75v where *possis* scored out and replaced with *possit*), but from fo. 82r to the end the lines are much closer together and the hand smaller, more or less as in the middle of CCCC. CCCC is probably earlier. Some of the handful of corrections in it are picked up in BL, e.g., CCCC p. 16, the repetition of *in manibus* does not appear in BL, fo. 80v, on p. 17 the replacement of *indulgentia* by *dipensatione* is in BL, and a deleted phrase farther down the page does not appear in BL. BL also has additions which improve the sense of CCCC, for example, the phrase *cum autem pluralitas beneficiorum* in BL, fo. 80v inserted in a passage in CCCC p. 16.

c) ASV, Arm. 32:34, fos. 480r-509, probably in a hand of the Gualteruzzi chancellery, very close to the printed text.

EDITIONS:
a) De concilio. De baptismo Constantini. Reformatio Angliae ex decretis eiusdem (Rome: Manuzio, 1562; reprint Farnborough, Hants.: Gregg Press, 1962);

b) Dillingen: S. Mayer, 1562;

c) Venice: G. Ziletti, 1562;

d) Rocaberti, pp. 350-64;

e) David Wilkins, ed., *Concilia magnae Britanniae et Hiberniae*, four volumes (London: Gosling et al., 1737), 4, pp. 121-26, collated from both the English MSS;

f) Sanctorum conciliorum et decretorum collectio nova... supplementum (Lucca: Giuseppe Salani and Vincenzo Giuntini, 1751), cc. 667-96 from Wilkins;

---

[188] *CRP*, no. 1538.

g) Mansi, 33, cc. 1109-1034 (from Labbé 1667; see no. 16 ab.);

h) Edward Cardwell, *Documentary Annals of the Reformed Church of England*, 2d edition, two volumes (Oxford: University Press, 1844), 1, pp. 143-61, from Wilkins, although without attribution;

i) T. E. Callahan, *Reginald, Cardinal Pole's Reformatio Angliae—a Critical Edition with Introduction and Commentary: A Thesis in History* (State University College at Buffalo, 1995);

j) Gerald Bray, ed., *The Anglican Canons* (Woodbridge: The Boydell Press and Church of England Record Society in association with the Ecclesiastical Law Society, 1998), pp. 69-137 (*Reformatio*), and 138-61 (collation of the two English MSS), both with English translation.

TRANSLATIONS:

a) Henry Raikes, *The Reformation of England, by the Decrees of Cardinal Pole* (Chester: R. H. Spence, 1839); *b)* Marmion, "London Synod," 2, pp. 1-65); c) Bray.

20) "Un comento sopra la sinodo fatta ultimamente nel regno d'Anglia" (title from ASV, Misc. Arm. II 79).

ATTESTATIONS: ASV, Misc. Arm. II 79, fo. 363r, no. 5; Pole to Scotti, 14-18 April 1556 (*CRP*, no. 1491); Beccadelli, no. 5?

DATE: after the last no.

MSS: none known, nor any text, unless this is a reference to the cover letter for the canons, printed at the front of *Reformatio Angliae*.

21) "De educanda Iuventute in disciplina ecclesiastica."

ATTESTATION: ASV, Misc. Arm. II 79, fo. 363r, no. 8. This work

Catalogue of Works

may be related to the possibly spurious treatise on the same topic which Pole is supposed to have solicited from his client Girolamo da Imola. I owe knowledge of Da Imola's "De recta studiorum Philosophie ratione . . . iussu Reginaldi Poli Cardinalisque scholis Angliae servanda proponent" to Daniel Brownstein, who could not, alas, remember where he had seen the reference.

DATE: During or after the London synod?

MS:
?Vat. lat. 5966, fos. 27r-31v. Title on separate page in large hand: "De educandis pueris." Heavily corrected. Autograph. Collation: fo. 29r at top "De modo et ratione educandi pueros destinatos ad clerum;" fos. 32r-4v another draft, "De modo et ratione educandi pueros qui ad clericatum vocantur;" most of 34v blank; fo. 36r probably a *disiectum membrum*; fos. 37r-47r are pieces of a treatise on the bishops, which may just possibly be a continuation of this, and perhaps also fos. 48r-63v and 64r-131v.
Edition: Brassel (1935), pp. 308-15 (fos. 32r-37r).

22) *De baptismo Constantini.*

ATTESTATIONS: *Nomenclator*; Torrigio; Freher; Wood, no. 9; Dodd, no. 9 (Rome, 1562, Louvain 1569); Tanner (Rome, Dillingen, and Venice, 1562; Louvain, 1567).

DATE: unknown.

MS: none known.
EDITIONS: a) as in Tanner; b) Rocaberti, pp. 346-49.

23) *Vita Longolii.*

ATTESTATIONS: Beccadelli (but not in the list of Pole's works); *Nomenclator*; Torrigio; Cooper; Klaiber, no. 2572.

DATE: before 1524.

MS: none known.
EDITION: *Christophori Longolii Orationes duae* (Florence: Heirs of F. Giunti, 1524; reprint Farnborough, Hants.: Gregg Press, 1967).

There is controversy over Pole's authorship.[189] The short biography first appeared anonymously in print as a preface to Longueil's *Orationes*, some two years after Longueil's death. Bernardo Giunti, the editor, described it simply as "a little commentary on the life of Christopher Longueil written by someone very friendly with him, who had lived familiarly with him" ("Christophori Longolii vitae commentariolum, ab amicissimo quodam eius, qui cum eo familiariter vixit conscriptum"). Not until Beccadelli's life of Pole was the *commentariolus* assigned to Pole. As George Parks pointed out, Beccadelli was not close to Pole at the time it was written.[190] In addition to the delayed attribution, Beccadelli implicitly downplayed the biography's importance, referring to it merely as an indication of what Pole was like when a student at Padua in the 1520s rather than including it in the roster of serious writing. Beccadelli may therefore not have been much concerned to establish the truth of his claim in the case of a work of minor significance.

Pole nevertheless looks a likely candidate because Longueil asked him, almost on his deathbed, "that, after my death, you lend your memory and goodwill humanly and piously to me as our close friendship demands" ("ut mortuo mihi memoriam benevolentiamque quam necessitudo nostra postulat humaniter ac pie praestes").[191] The *Vita* contains a very similar passage, in

---

[189] Most recently, Jonathan Woolfson writes that "it seems probable" that the work is Pole's. *Padua and the Tudors: English Students in Italy, 1485-1603* (Toronto: University of Toronto Press, 1998), p. 111.

[190] George B. Parks, "Did Pole write the 'Vita Longolii?'" *Renaissance Quarterly*, 26 (1973): 274-85, p. 279.

[191] *CRP*, no. 14; cf. Parks, p. 275. Alessandro Pastore accepts Pole's authorship, but claims on unknown evidence that Bembo and Leonico collaborated.

which Longueil appointed Pole his executor so that Pole "should have his reputation and memory dear" ("famamque suam & memoriam charam haberet").[192] This trick of converting the direct discourse of a letter into third-person narration was frequently employed by the authors of the first two lives of Pole. But the end of the *Vita* also makes the most trouble for Pole's authorship. Not only does it refer to Pole twice in the third person, but in one of these instances Pole was described as having "lived [with Longueil] to the end of his life, most closely linked in letters" ("coniunctissime in literis usque ad extremum vitae diem vixit"), which might appear to be unseemly bragging.[193]

Two extrinsic reasons have been offered for doubting Pole's authorship. One especially heavily emphasized is that neither Pole's client Thomas Lupset when announcing the *Vita* to Erasmus, nor Erasmus himself in his discussion of contemporary Ciceronians identified Pole as the writer.[194] It has also been pointed out that in a 1530 letter Pierre Bunel reported that "[n]either [Giovanni Battista] Egnazio nor he who supervised the printing of Longueil's letters [Giunti himself?] has a specific person in mind as the author of the 'Vita Longolii'....I have met some who surmise that Villeneuve was the author. Since our knowledge is incomplete, I do not think that it can reasonably be attributed to anyone with certainty."[195] One critic has made much of the possible attribution to Simon de Villeneuve, but nevertheless decided that it really does not make much difference and Pole could after all have done the deed. These points have force

---

Alessandro Pastore, "Due bibliote che umanistiche del Cinquecento (I libri del cardinal Pole e di Marcantonio Flaminio)," *Rinascimento*, ser. 2, 19 (1979): 269-90, p. 271n.4.

[192] *Vita*, in *Christophori Longolii Orations duae* (Florence: Giunti, 1524; reprinted Farnborough, Hants.: Gregg Press, 1967), sig. 8r. Cf. Parks, "*Vita Longolii*," p. 28

[193] Parks, "*Vita Longolii*," pp. 282-3.

[194] Parks, "*Vita Longolii*," pp. 276-7. Parks added more supposition about mysterious incognito visits to Basel to reinforce his point.

[195] Quoted in Alvin Vos, "The *Vita Longolii*: Additional Considerations about Reginald Pole's Authorship," *Renaissance Quarterly*, 30 (1977): 324-33, p. 324.

only if we assume that Pole, always the reluctant author, would have let anyone know of his role.

Egnazio is the pivotal figure in both the argument for Villeneuve and its modification in favor of maybe Pole after all. Egnazio might deserve that prominence, although I have yet to find any direct links between him and Pole. They surely must have known each other, given the Englishmen he taught in Padua and Egnazio's close friendship with Contarini.[196] If his knowledge is important, it might be because both he and Bunel at some time shared religious views with Pole, but not at precisely the right time to support the case against Pole's authorship. Bunel for his part five years after the letter about the *Vita* praised Pole as one "who esteems all human things less than Christ. Although he excels in philosophy and eloquence, he does not wish to imitate those who think they are not Ciceronian enough if they address Christ by name, or not philosophical enough if they think well of piety. . . .Pole, who is the most learned, pleasant, and upright person I know, is totally involved in the study of [Christ]."[197]

Bunel, who had by then returned to France in the service of Georges de Selve, bishop of Lavaur, wrote much the same thing directly to Pole in 1539.[198] Bunel's judgment looks solid, and may offer a motive for Pole's reluctance to acknowledge the work. He always had trouble disgorging his works, and he might have been doubly reluctant in the case of the *Vita* since most of its content and all of its form and language contradicted the views he had come to hold. This is all supposition, but it can safely be said that none of the arguments against Pole's authorship is any more solid.

An identikit of the author can be built up from the five uses

---

[196] Thomas F. Mayer, *Thomas Starkey and the Commonweal: Humanist Politics and Religion in the Reign of Henry VIII* (Cambridge: Cambridge University Press, 1989), pp. 44, 54-5, 197, 229 and Eugenio Massa, *L'eremo, la Bibbia e il Medioevo in Umanisti veneti del primo Cinquecento* (Naples: Liguori, 1992), passim.

[197] Quoted in Vos, "*Vita Longolii*," p. 332, his translation.

[198] *CRP*, no. 249.

Catalogue of Works

of the first person in the *Vita*.[199] Of these, the first, noting Longueil's powerful memory, is of no particular consequence, nor is the fifth on his generosity. But numbers 2, 3 and 4 seem to me to point much more squarely at Pole than at anyone else. Longueil's interest in Pliny is exactly parallel to Pole's in Galen.[200] Bembo's prominence in modifying Longueil's style again cuts especially close to a northerner like Pole. It is possible that Pole's protégé Thomas Starkey chose to write in English on Bembo's advice.[201] Finally, the emphasis on Longueil's relations with English scholars during his trip to Britain probably points to an English author, as well Pole as any of the other candidates.

The best way to settle the issue might be to compare the prose of the *Vita* to Pole's few letters contemporary with it. I am very grateful to Diana Robin for undertaking that task. She found marked similarities, including stock Ciceronian patterns of subordination, a predilection for the pluperfect subjunctive in subordinate clauses, and for pairing and parallelism, but she also noted that the prose of both was so formulaic that virtually any cadet Ciceronian could have written it in his sleep. Nevertheless, even absent conclusive results of an investigation into style, I see no compelling reason to reject Beccadelli's claim, the more so in that there is an odd consistency in Pole's writing of biographies of his dead friends which supports other grounds for his authorship.[202] That Pole's familiar Gentian Hervet copied Longueil's commentaries on Cicero while in Pole's household, while not perhaps adding much to the case for Pole's authorship of the *Vita*, does confirm Pole's wish to keep Longueil's memory alive, and

---

[199] Parks, "Vita Longolii," pp. 280-82.

[200] As Woolfson, *Padua*, pp. 92-3 also observes. See further his "John Claymond, Pliny the Elder, and the Early History of Corpus Christi College, Oxford," *English Historical Review*, 112 (1997): 882-903.

[201] Mayer, *Starkey*, p. 66.

[202] Except for the references which point to an English author, Gregorio Cortese might also be a candidate. Longueil's death upset him greatly, and one of his letters amounts to a capsule biography. *Gregorii Cortesii monachi casinatis S. R. E. cardinalis omnia quae huc usque colligi potuerunt, sive ab eo scripta, sive ad illum spectantia*, two volumes (Padua: Giuseppe Comino, 1774), 2, pp. 104-5.

may mean that he at one time meant to include the commentaries in the 1524 edition of Longueil's works.[203] It may have been Hervet's MS that was still in Pole's library in 1555, or it may have been one of two sets of Longueil's original marginalia to an unidentified edition of Cicero's philosophical works, or to his *Opera rhetorica: oratoria et forensia* (Paris: Jean Petit, 1511) now in the New College, Oxford, library.[204]

The *Vita* concluded with a long passage stressing Pole's intimacy with and solicitude for Longueil. This is one of the points which has been thought to make against Pole's authorship. I think, on the contrary, that it almost clinches the affirmative case, if for no other reason than that Pole used exactly the same ploy in *De unitate*. When he first introduced the martyrs Fisher and More, he emphasized that they were "of all the dearest friends to me" ("mihi amicos omnium charissimos").[205] The claim to close friendship could not have been literally true. However much Pole thought of More, there is very little sign of intimacy between them, and in Fisher's case, there seems to be no evidence whatever of a relationship to Pole.[206]

24) Psalms commentaries.

ATTESTATIONS: Beccadelli, no. 6; Dudic, no. 12 ("in Davidis hymnos"); Wood, no. 14 (same title); Tanner; Cooper, who listed

---

[203] *Gentiani Herveti Aurelii quaedam opsucula* (Louvain: Etienne Dolet, 1541), p. 45.

[204] Pastore, "Due biblioteche," pp. 280 ("Cic[eronis] op[er]a p[hilo]s[oph]ica cu[m] annot[ationibus] Longolii"), which Pastore was unable to locate and p. 281 "Cic[eronis] op[era] oratoria cum annot[ationibus] Longol[ii]," now New College, Oxford, shelfmark Ω.15.3., citing A. B. Emden, "Longolius's collection of books," in P. S. Allen, H. M. Allen and H. W. Garrod, eds., *Opus epistolarum Desiderii Erasmi roterodami* (Oxford: Clarendon Press, 1905-58), 11, p. 382. Pole must therefore certainly have known some of Longueil's commentaries, against Parks, "Vita Longolii," pp. 277-78. Longueil's notes were not published until 1582.

[205] *Reginaldi Poli ad Henricum octavum Britanniae regem, pro ecclesiasticae unitatis defensione* (Rome: Antonio Blado, [1539]), fo. XXXr.

[206] For More, see *Prince and Prophet*, chapter one, and chapter two for Pole's sponsoring of at least one and perhaps two lives of Fisher.

Catalogue of Works

it among MSS at Douai.

DATE: unknown.

MSS:
Vat. lat. 5969, fo. 1v headed "Fragmentum Adnotationum in quosdam Psalmos."

a) fos. 1br-48r. Collation: fo. 1br "4" in lower left; also numbered 27-75 in upper right. A few corrections, perhaps in same hand as in Vat. lat. 5967, fos. 296ff (*CRP*, no. 573). Main text looks like Holland's hand.

b) fos. 55r-118r. Title on 53r: "Super Psalmum Venite exaltemus." Brown paper makes much of the text illegible.

c) fos. 122r-32v. Another version. Autograph draft. Mainly clear.

d) fos. 133ff. Continued? Some brown paper. In.: "Se intelligere ostendere. M. Sic presente fit omnes M. eum deteliquerint." Ex.: illegible.

25) "Un trattato sopra il sermone del S.re in Monte."

ATTESTATION: ASV, Misc. Arm. II 79, fo. 363r, no. 4.

DATE: unknown.

MS: Vat. lat. 5969, fos. 174r-290v, "De Sermone Domini in monte dialogus." In.: illegible. Ex.: "Credo in Jesum Christum dominum nostrum." Brown paper and very faint.

26) "In Canticum B. Mariae."

ATTESTATION: none.

DATE: unknown.

MS: Vat. lat. 5968, fos. 365rff, nearly all illegible. Probably related to the sermon in St. Mary-Arches (ab. no. 10a), and perhaps not an independent work.

27) "Commentarios in Esaiam."

ATTESTATIONS: Dudic no. 11; Wood, no. 13; Tanner; included under Beccadelli, no. 6?; Cooper, among MSS at Douai.

DATE: unknown.

MS: none known.

28) Other scripture commentaries.

ATTESTATIONS: Dudic, no. 13 (said to be in poor shape); Dodd, no. 19 ("Comment. in varios scrip. sacr. libros. Opus imperfectum. MS."). According to Alfonso Chacón (c. 638), Pole also translated Jeremiah's "Lamentations" from Hebrew, but it is hard to say what this reference means.

DATE: unknown.

MSS:
on Acts
Vat. lat. 5969:
   a) fos. 293r-312v. Title fo. 292r: "In librum Actorum Apostolorum usque ad iii cap. manu D. Card. sunt fol. Xi (?) No. 9 ["15" *del.*] Select."
   b) fos. 316r-28r. Title fo. 314r: "No. 10 in Acta Apostolorum ["alia" *del.*] explanatio usque ad tertium capitulum. Quint. 2 manu D. Sethi." "In primum caput actuum [sic] apostolorum praefatio."
   c) Vat. lat. 5970.2, fo. 313r. Title: "In Epistolas Pauli ad Romanos 32. [*del.*]," but no text extant.
   d) Vat. lat. 5968, index, gives "De institutione sacrarum

super 3. cap. evangelistarum Matthei 26. Marci 14. Lucae 27.," but no text extant.

29) "Catechismus."

Attestations: Dudic, no. 14; Wood, no. 15; Dodd, no. 20 (combined with the next into "Catechismus de passione Christi. Opus imperfectum. MS"); Tanner; Cooper, among MSS at Douai; ?Klaiber, no. 2575, *An uniforme and Catholyke Primer* (London: J. Waylande, 1555). Cf. Also no. 29 below.

MSS: none known, and there is no evidence linking Pole to any known catechism, except Carranza's, which he wished to have translated into English.[207] The primer cited by Klaiber is not a catechism, but rather one of a number of editions of the Use of Sarum which included catechetical sections. See the discussion in Edgar Hoskins, *Horae Beatae Mariae Virginis or Sarum and York Primers and Primers of the Reformed Roman Use* (London: Longmans, Green, & Co., 1901), pp. 71-81 and 186-90 for a description of this specific version (STC, no. 16060). Its title says only that it was "newly set forth by certayne of the cleargy with the assente of the moste reverende father in god the Lorde Cardinall Pole hys grace," not that it was in any sense Pole's work. Nevertheless, it is important to observe that he did approve this quasi-catechetical book, although Mary beat him to the punch with a patent for its printing (printed after the colophon) issued before Pole returned to England. For some reason, Wayland's numerous reprintings did not bear the statement of Pole's approbation.

30) "De Passione Christi Dialogus."

ATTESTATIONS: Dudic, no. 15; Wood, no. 16; Dodd, no. 20 (cf. last entry); Tanner; Cooper, among MSS at Douai.

DATE: unknown, although this may have been written as consolation on Flaminio's death in 1550.

---

[207] *CRP*, no. 2252

MS: Vat. lat. 5969:

a) fos. 333r-50v. "Dialogo imperfecto de passione Christi et quo pacto fructus praecipui possit ex eius celebratione in (?) eiusdem exemplum adiectum." "No. 35" left margin below title. Right margin: "manu D. Car. fol. 10;" mid-page "Select." Large "3" upper left corner. In.: "Studeo ex te nunc [*ab.*] aliquid audire quod me q [*del.*] commone [sic] faciat quopacto iis [*del.*] ea legens vel audiens quae iis feriis quibus." Ex.: "quasi crucem ante oculos haberet et quereret locum ubi se a (?) dei absconderet: quod Christus non fecit." Collation: fo. 333r left bottom corner "A;" fo. 335 "B;" fo. 337 has marginal note—no apparent "C" under it—ergo this collation added?; fo. 339 "D;" fo. 341 "E;" fo. 343 "F;" rest blank. No other foliation/pagination.

b) fos. 353r-364r. Fair copy, in first hand of "De reformatione." In.: "Studeo ex te nunc aliquid audire, quod me commone [sic] faciat, quo pacto ea legens vel audiens, quae iis feriis." Ex.: "In summa si bene consideres vitam istorum qui se reges faciunt, horum statum."

31) "Anglice Orationem, quam ad Concilium totius Regni Angliae tum habuit, cum id Regnum ad Ecclesiae unitatem revocatum est."

ATTESTATIONS: Dudic, no. 18; Wood, no. 3; Dodd, no. 3 (probably taken from Foxe); Tanner.

DATE: Wood, Dodd and Tanner all give the date as 27 November 1554, probably all drawing on Foxe, but this must be a mistake for the 28th, given correctly in Dudic (see e) bel.).

MSS:
Vat. lat. 5968:

a) fos. 305r-59r, "Ad concilium parliamenti." Scribal copy (reading text?). Collation: original foliation 1-55.

b) fos. 129r-45v. Autograph draft.

c) fos. 361r-76v, "no. 4 Ad consilium parlamenti." Draft with some autograph corrections.

d) Cf. another, much briefer, speech to Parliament in Italian in ASV, Segreteria di Stato, Inghilterra 3, fos. 156r-8v, dated 28

November 1554 (cf. Latin version in ASV, Fondo Borghese I, 976, fo. 17 "Minuta di una oratione inedita del cardinale Reginald Polo ad Britanniae populum habita con giunte e correctioni autografe dello stesso cardinale"); in unknown hand, unless perhaps Holland hurrying. Endorsed "Card. Oratio," in what may be one of the hands in the Vat. lat. *Nachlass*. Headed in the same hand as text "Reginald Poli card. Oratio ad Britanniae populum habita."

e) CCCC, MS 101, no. 22, a short fragment.

f) Roger Ascham translated the speech for Julius III, pleasing Pole, but the manuscript owned by Ascham's biographer Grant has apparently disappeared.[208]

EDITIONS:

a) Elder, *Copie of a letter*, sigs. Div-Eiir; reprinted in John Foxe, *Actes and monuments of matters most speciall and memorable* (London: John Day, 1583; *STC* no. 11225), pp. 1476-7 (cf. S. R. Catteley, ed., *The Acts and Monuments of John Foxe*, 6 [London: Seeley and Burnside, 1838], pp. 568-71) and *The Chronicle of Queen Jane, and of Two Years of Queen Mary* (Camden Society, 1st ser., 48, 1850), pp. 136-66, pp. 154-59;

b) Il felicissimo ritorno del regno d'Inghilterra alla catholica unione, & alla obedientia della sede apostolica (Rome, s. a.), reprinted in *ERP*, 4, pp. 312-13;

c) [Matthew Parker?], *De antiquitate britannicae ecclesiae*, pp. 415-16 in Latin and indirect discourse, but likely a translation from Elder;

d) in English in Francis Thynne's life of Pole in Raphael Hollinshead, *Chronicles of England, Scotland and Ireland*, six volumes (London: J. Johnson, et al., 1807-1808), 4, pp. 753-54 and in ibid., 4, pp. 65-66, probably both translated from Parker;

e) Dudic, *ERP*, 1, pp. 34-5;

f) Calendar...Simancas, 13, no. 127;

g) Juan Ginés Sepulveda, *Opera, cum edita, tum inedita*, ed. Regia historiae academia, two volumes (Madrid: La Gazeta, 1780), 2, pp. 505-7, paraphrase in Latin, independent of *c)*, which

---

[208] Lawrence Ryan, *Roger Ascham* (Stanford: Stanford University Press, 1963), p. 208.

does not include the last, inflammatory part of the speech, in which Pole compared Charles to David and Philip to Solomon; [209] *CRP,* no. 991 (summary).

32) Canterbury visitation articles.

ATTESTATIONS: Tanner; Klaiber, no. 2577 (Canterbury: D. Michel, 1556), a slightly garbled version of *STC* no. 10149 (Canterbury: J. Michel [1556]).

DATE: Probably those of 1556, rather than Archdeacon Harpsfield's of 1557 are meant.[210]

MS: LPL, Arch. Reg., fos. 34v-5v, "Articuli inquirendi in visitatione."
EDITIONS: 1556 as ab.; Strype, *Ecclesiastical Memorials,* 3:1, pp. 291-93; W. H. Frere and W. M. Kennedy, eds., *Visitation Articles & Injunctions of the Period of the Reformation,* three volumes (New York: Alcuin Club, 1910), 2, pp. 385-91; slightly imperfect in Tellechea Idigoras, *Carranza y Pole,* pp. 350-51.

33) "De prudentia et sapientia humana et ea quae per Christum humano genere misericordia dei fuit revelata."

ATTESTATION: none.

DATE: unknown. The hand seems early, and it is possible that the work dates from 1537.

MS: Vat. lat. 5966, fos. 3r-26r. Autograph.

---

[209] Cf. Glyn Redworth, "'Matters impertinent to women:' Male and female monarchy under Philip and Mary," *English Historical Review,* 112, no. 447 (June 1997), pp. 597-613, p. 610.

[210] For Harpsfield's articles see L. E. Whatmore, ed., *Archdeacon Harpsfield's Visitation, 1557,* 1 (Catholic Record Society, 45, 1950).

34) Letter to Julius III on abbey lands, 30 November 1554.

ATTESTATIONS: De Frede, p. 67; Wood, no. 3 ("touching the restoring of the realm of England"); Dodd, no. 5 (probably taken from Foxe); Tanner ("de reformatione Angliae"); perhaps the letter cited in Vat. lat. 12909, fos. 160r-65r from a printed source in the BAV (probably one of the numerous editions of e) bel.); Klaiber, no. 2573.

MSS:

a) Vat. lat. 5967, fos. 376r-77r, minute in Faita's hand with autograph corrections, headed in Binardi's hand "Iulio iii. ex Anglia, Londino. 30 Novembris 1554."

b) Vat lat. 5827, fos. 18r-20r.

c) BNM, MS Lat. XI. no. 60 (6527), fos. 216v-17r.

d) Padua, Biblioteca del Seminario, MS 71, fos. 77v-79v (16th-century copy).

e) ASV, Nunz. div. 145, fos. 183v-7r, dated 1553 (eighteenth-century copy).

f) Folger Shakespeare Library, Washington, W. b. 132 (78) (Strozzi transcripts), fos. 137r-9v, dated 1553.

g) ASV, Fondo Borghese II, 483 B, fos. 158r-61r, dated 1553.

h) ASV, Fondo Carpegna 202, fos. 127r-28v (copied in BL, Add. MS 15388, fo. 329r-v).

i) Barb. lat. 5354, fos. 18v-20v.

EDITIONS:

a) Copia delle lettere del Sereniss. Re d'Inghilterra, & del Reverendiss. Card. Polo Legato...alla Santità di N. S. Iulio Papa III (Rome: Valerio & Luigi Dorici, 1554?);

b) also Milan, according to Klaiber;

c) Natale Conti, *Universae historiae sui temporis libri triginta ab anno salutis nostrae 1545 usque ad annum 1581* (Venice: Damiano Zenaro, 1581), pp. 181-82 (no indication of source);

d) translated in Foxe, ed. Cattley, 6, pp. 573-4 (reprinted from earlier edition of Foxe in Wilkins, ed., *Concilia*, 4, pp. 110-11);

e) Cesare Baroni, ed. Oderico Rinaldi, *Annales ecclesiastici*, thirty-four volumes (Paris: Consociatio Sancti Pauli, 1880), 33, cc. 499-500;

    f) reprinted from an earlier edition of Rinaldi in *ERP*, 5, pp. 129-31;

    g) *CRP*, no. 993 (summary).

35) "Apologia ad Paulum IV."

ATTESTATIONS: Dudic (but not in list of works); Tellechea, ed. *Doc. Hist.*, 2, pp. 512 (testimony of Juan de Villagarcia), 897 (Feria) and 884 (Bernardo Fresneda); cf. *Carranza y Pole*, pp. 140-41 and p. 278; Mercati, "I costituti," p. 181.

DATE: late summer 1557. Pole's chronology of events in the "Apologia" is confused, but most of the events mentioned point to the time of writing as August or September.

MS: Inner Temple Library, London, Petyt MS 538/46, fos. 391r-426v, probably in Faita's hand. Collation: fo. 410 repeated twice and 416 once; originally foliated 1-36. The first two leaves and the final three lack an original foliation. Half of fo. 411v is blank, and fo. 412r starts with the same sentence as on mid-411v.
EDITIONS:

    a) J. I. Tellechea Idigoras, "Pole y Paolo IV. Una célebre apología inédita del cardenal Inglés (1557)," *Archivum Historiae Pontificiae*, 4 (1966), pp. 105-54, pp. 133-54;

    b) Joseph Fischer, "Essai Historique sur les Idées Réformatrices des Cardinaux Jean Pierre Carafa (1476-1559) et Reginald Pole (1500-1558)," thesis for the Faculté de Théologie de Paris, 1957, pp. 14-34 according to Romeo De Maio, *Riforme e miti nella Chiesa del Cinquecento* (Naples: Guida Editori, 1973), p. 84n (I have been unable to see Fischer's work);

    c) *CRP*, no. 2076 (summary).

36) Exhortation to the council of Trent.

Probably the opening sermon is meant.
ATTESTATIONS: Torrigio; Ghilini; Tanner.

Catalogue of Works

DATE: Before 7 February 1546.[211]

MSS:
According to *CT*, 4, they are (all given without folio numbers):
  a) ASV, Carte Farnesiane, 6;
  b) ASV, Concilio tridentino, 62; and
  c) ASV, Concilio tridentino, 123.

EDITIONS:
  a) Admonitio atque hortatio legatorum sedis apostolicae ad Patres in Concilio Tridentino lecta in prima sessione (Rome: In platea Parionis, 1546), fos. 5r-8v, copy in ASV, Conc. Trid., 98; *CT* gives
  b) Venice: Vincenzo Valgrisio, 1546;
  c) CT 4, pp. 548-53.

TRANSLATION:
Vincent McNabb, *Cardinal Pole's Legatine Address at the Opening of the Council of Trent, 7 January 1546* (London: Burns, Oates, Washburne, 1936).

37) An edition of Cicero?

ATTESTATIONS: Wood, no. 21 ("various readings, emendations, castigations, etc. of Cicero's works"); Dodd, no. 13 ("Collections and various readings from Cicero's works").

MSS: none known. It is possible that this is a mistaken reference to Longueil's notes on Cicero's oratorical works, of which Pole had charge, and which à Wood could have seen in the library of New College, Oxford.[212]

38) Divorce opinion.

ATTESTATIONS: Wood, no. 22 (from John Strype, *Memorials of the*

---

[211] *CT*, 2, p.415.

[212] See note 199.

Most Reverend Father in God Thomas Cranmer, 2, first published in 1694, who doubted its authenticity); Tanner, citing the same source.

DATE: Before 13 June 1531, the date of Cranmer's summary.

MS: BL, Lansdowne 115, fos. 2r-3r.
EDITION: Nicholas Pocock, ed., *Records of the Reformation. The Divorce, 1527-1533*, two volumes (Oxford: Clarendon Press, 1870), 2, pp. 130-31.

39) Statuta academiae Cantabrigiensis.

ATTESTATION: Tanner, citing CCCC, misc. x. p. 83.

DATE: 18 March 1557.

MS: CCCC, MS 118 no. 8, with copy of first section only in no. 9; Oxford, Bodleian Library, Tanner MS 156, fos. 60r-84v.

EDITIONS: a) John Lamb, ed., *A Collection of Letters, Statutes and Other Documents from the Manuscript Library of Corpus Christi College, Illustrative of the History of the University of Cambridge* (London: John W. Parker, 1838), pp. 237-55 (partially);
    b) *CRP*, no. 1911 (summary).

40) *Consilium de emendanda ecclesia.*

ATTESTATIONS: Nicholas Pseaume's diary entry under date of 17 September 1563, where the work is largely attributed to Pole;[213] Torrigio; Ghilini; Freher.

DATE: 1538.
EDITIONS:
    a) Cologne: no publisher, 1538;
    b) reprinted Mansi, 32, cc. 348-55;

---

[213] *CT*, 2, p. 871. For Pseaume (1518-1575), see pp. cxlvii-cliv.

c) reprinted B. J. Kidd, ed., *Documents Illustrative of the Continental Reformation* (Oxford: Clarendon Press, 1911);

d) *Consilium delectorum cardinalium et aliorum praelatorum. . .libellus vere aureus, ante annos 70. in Concil. Tridentino primum editus, deinde Romani Antichristi tyrannico iussu iniuste suppressus* (London: Felix Kingston, 1609), printed from a copy belonging to William Crashaw;

e) *CT,* 12, pp. 131-45.

TRANSLATIONS:

a) Martin Luther, *Ratschlag eins ausschus etlicher Cardinel, Bapst Paulo des names dem dritten, auff seinem befehl geschrieben und uberantwortet* (Wittenberg: Hans Lufft, 1538);

b) Elisabeth G. Gleason, *Reform Thought in Sixteenth-Century Italy* (Chico, Calif.: Scholars Press, 1981; American Academy of Religion, Texts and Translations Series, ed., James A. Massey, 4), pp. 81-100.

41) A dialogue with Elizabeth I about "cosas de la fe."

ATTESTATION: Feria said Elizabeth had sent him all the papers she had from Pole, but he thought that at least this dialogue had been excluded.[214] Gregorio Leti included in his *Historia overo Vita di Elisabetha, Regina d'Inghilterra* what he said was a printed dialogue between Pole and Elizabeth, dated 1555. Leti researched his book in England where he had access to at least one of the best libraries, that of the Earl of Anglesey, as well as to Bishop Burnet, then in the process of writing his *History of the Reformation,* so it may be that this is an authentic work, now lost. It does not appear in the sale catalogue of Angelsey's library.[215]

---

[214] Tellechea, ed., *Doc. Hist.,* 2, p. 897.

[215] Gregorio Leti, *Historia overo Vita di Elisabetta, Regina d'Inghilterra* (Amsterdam: Abraham Wolfgang, 1693), preface for Anglesey. His library numbered well over 5,000 volumes according to the auction catalogue, *Bibliotheca Angleseiana, sive Catalogus Variorum librorum in quavis lingua, & facultate insignium* (London: per Thomam Philippum, 1686). Cf. also John Lawler, *Book Auctions in England in the Seventeenth Century (1676-1700)* (London: Eliot Stock, 1898), p. xxxvi. For Leti's time in England, see especially

MS: none known.
EDITION: Leti, *Vita di Elisabetta*, 1, pp. 280-90.[216]

Spurious or doubtful works

42) *Tractatus de justificatione.*

ATTESTATIONS: Pitts; Torrigio; Ghilini; Freher (all three say it was written in English and Ghilini and Torrigio identify it as a translation of the sixth session of Trent); Wood, no. 19; Dodd, no. 11 (Louvain, 1569) and no. 12; Tanner ("Inveniebantur manu cardinalis scripti in custodia camerarii sui Henrici Pyning," Louvain, 1569); Cooper. For the debate over the authenticity of this work, see Dermot Fenlon's summary.[217] He rejects Pole's authorship largely on the grounds of the work's form and the circumstances of its publication which served the need of Pole's fellow Catholic exiles at Louvain to portray him as doctrinally sound. But Pole's willingness to submit "De summo pontifice" to the correction of two famously scholastic Louvain theologians may mean that he was prepared to change his approach and suggest that the *Tractatus* should be attributed to him.[218] Then again, Tapper had been involved in an acrimonious dispute with Pole's ally, Pedro de Soto, whom he tried to delate to the Inquisition in Flanders and Spain, and it was rumored that Pole and others were joining Soto in a rejoinder.[219] It may be that some of Tapper's animus arose from the fact that he thought Pole had treated him frivolously over *De summo pontifice*. The most

---

Luigi Fassò, *Avventurieri della penna del Seicento* (Florence: Le Monnier, 1923), pp. 165-209.

[216] Franco Barcia, *Bibliografia delle opere di Gregorio Leti* (Milan: Franco Angeli, 1981), pp. 417-19 for a summary of the editions, treated at greater length thereafter. See also Franco Barcia, *Un politico dell'eta barocca, Gregorio Leti* (Milan: Franco Angeli, 1983).

[217] Fenlon, *Heresy and Obedience*, pp. 198-99.

[218] See ab., p. 25.

[219] Tellechea, ed., *Doc. Hist.*, 2, pp. 531; 563-64; 883-4.

detailed treatment is Bruskewitz, *Theology of Justification*, which unquestioningly accepts the work as Pole's.

MSS: none known.
EDITION:
Treatie of Iustification (Louvain: John Fowler, 1569). According to the title page it was "founde emong the writings of Cardinal Pole of blessed memorie, remaining in the custodie of M. Henri Pyning, Chamberlaine and General Receiver to the said Cardinal, late deceased in Lovaine. Item, certain translations touching the said matter of *Iustification*."[220]

43) *A brefe overture or openyng of the legacion of... Cardinall Poole...with the substance of his oracyon to the Kyng & Quenes Majestie, for the reconcilement of the Realme of Englande to the unities of the Catholyke Churche*

[1555?]. Cited in Lee, p. 255, but it does not appear in the *STC*.

44) Translations of sermons of Chrysostom, Basil, Cyprian, and Leo, concerning fasting, alms, and prayer.

ATTESTATIONS: Wood, no. 19, who correctly includes them with the *Treatie of justification*; Dodd, no. 15 says they were MSS; Tanner.
EDITION: Cf. No. 42

45) "The Sarum Missal, breviary, ritual, etc. revised and published by him, 1554, 1555."

ATTESTATION: Dodd, no. 21.
Cf. no. 29 ab. For an edition of the Sarum Use authorized, but no more, by Pole. All the missals proper listed in STC, nos. 16215-18 are supposed to be reprints of the 1534 ed. (No. 16214). No. 16217, the only one I was able to check, was printed in Paris by Guillaume Merlin in 1555 and makes no mention of Pole.

---

[220] Cf. Southern, *Recusant Prose*, p. 479.

Marmion could not find any copies of the missal which "show directly the influence of the London synod," and the same is true of the primers.[221] The one with Pole's imprimatur was published on 4 June 1555, before the synod met. A copy in the British Library is supposed to have belonged to Pole, and may have come from Douai via St. Edmund's College, Ware.[222]

46) Miscellaneous (a very unhelpful indication!).

ATTESTATION: Dudic, no. 16.

47) "Libellus item de natali die Christi, Servatoris [sic] nostri."

ATTESTATIONS: Dudic, no. 9; Wood, no. 12; Dodd, no. 18; Tanner; Cooper, among MSS at Douai; Klaiber, no. 2578 (Canterbury, 1557, but almost certainly a mistaken reading from Zimmermann).

MSS: none known. This may be a mistaken reference to part of "Sopra la Rosa et la Spada et il Capello" (no. 13 ab.).

48) "Proposita a D. Carli. Paulo iii de rebus Anglicis cum mitturus esset legatos de pace ad principes."

ATTESTATION: Vat. lat. 5970.2, fo. 419r. "No. 55 ["5" *ov.* "0"], Select." The content makes it clear that this work is not by Pole.

MSS: Vat. lat. 5971, fos. 60ar-60ev (new 63r-67v, formerly 420r-24v of Vat. lat. 5970). In.: "Quia supplicanti mihi pro causa Regni Angliae, ut Reverendissimis Legatis inter alia mandata." Ex.: "qui in omnibus, ut debeo, meum iudicium quamhumillime submitto."
EDITION: *ERP*, 5, pp. 150-7.

---

[221] Marmion, "London Synod," 2, p. 76.

[222] Ibid., p. 74.

49) *De potestate ecclesiastica.*

ATTESTATION: *Nomenclator.* Both *De summo pontifice* and *De concilio* are also in this catalogue, so this reference cannot be a mistake for them.

50) *De modo orandi.*

ATTESTATION: *Nomenclator.* This could be a mistake for "De modo concionandi."

INDEX

Agustín, Antonio, 80, 81
Annesley, Arthur, Earl of Anglesey, 107
"Apology" to Pope Paul, 10
Aristotle, 2
Ascham, Roger, 101
Avignon, 2

Bartoli, Bernardo de', 75
Basil, 109
Beccadelli, Ludovico, 12, 17, 20, 21, 24, 27, 28, 29, 54, 92, 95
Becket, Thomas, 4
Bembo, Pietro, 2, 5, 95
Benci, Trifone, 44
Beneficio di Christo, 4
Binardi, Gianbattista, 16-18, 20, 26, 29, 31, 35, 55, 57, 61, 62, 68, 81, 103
Bobadilla, Nicolás, 74
Bologna, 37
Bonamico, Lazzaro, 27
Bonelli, Michele, 29
Bonner, Edmund, 73
Borromeo, Carlo, 9
Brassel, Paul, 11
Bristol, 77
Brussels, 19, 24
Bunau, Heinrich de, 50
Bunel, Pierre, 93-95
Buonarotti, Michelangelo, 4
Burnet, Gilbert, 107

Calvin, 4, 10
Canossa, Matteo, 44
Canterbury, 4, 9
Carafa, Antonio, 35-38
Carafa, Gianpietro, 6, 7, 10, 21, 22, 23, 26, 40
Carnesecchi, Pietro, 4, 18, 20, 21, 29

Carpentras, 2
Carranza, Bartolomé, 9, 87, 99
Carter, William, 58
Casale, Francesco Andrea de, 37
Castelvetro, Ludovico, 57
Cawarden, Sir Thomas, 87
Chacón, Alfonso, 98
Charles V, 2, 3, 5, 7, 39, 47, 48, 53, 82, 85, 101
Charles XII, 49
Cheke, Sir John, 9
Chrysostom, John, 109
Cicero, Marcus Tullius, 96, 105
Cobelluzzi, Scipione, 35, 39
Colonna, Vittoria, 4, 75, 84
Comitoli, Napoleone, 35, 36, 37, 38
Consilium de emendanda ecclesia, 3, 106
Constantine, Emperor, 5
Contarini, Alvise, 26, 39, 78
Contarini, Gasparo, 3, 5, 43, 74, 94
Contarini, Giacomo, 59
Contarini, Girolamo, 34
Contarini, Pietro Francesco, 59, 60
Contarini, Placido, 27
Cope, Alan, 58
Cosimo I de' Medici, Duke of Florence, 6, 21
Cranmer, Thomas, 8-9, 56, 69, 70, 77, 105
Crome, Edward, 9
Cromwell, Thomas, 3
Cyprian, 109

Dahlberg, John Edward, Baron Acton, 74
Da Mula, Marcantonio, 60
Daniel, penitentiary, 45
David, 101
De concilio, 5

Index

Della Rovere, Giulio, 6, 36, 76
Della Torre, Francesco, 44
De Luca, Giuseppe, 14, 49
"De modo concionandi," 16
"De reformatione ecclesiae," 30
De sacramento, 9, 21
De summo pontifice, 6, 24
De unitate, 2, 4, 5, 10, 11
Dillingen, 25, 77
Di pace, 8
Dixon, Richard Watson, 57
Douai, 13
Dudic, Andras, 12, 16, 24, 27, 28, 29, 33, 42, 48, 55, 62, 63, 76, 100
Dunn, Thomas F., 44

Edward VI, 13
Egnazio, Giovanni Battista, 93, 94
Elizabeth I, 33, 107
Elton, Sir Geoffrey, 4
Erasmus, Desiderius, 93
Ercolani, Vincenzo, 36

Facchetto, Michele, 32
Fairhurst papers, Lambeth Palace Library, 58
Faita, Marcantonio, 16, 20, 24, 26, 29, 31, 48, 57, 62, 63, 64, 68, 71, 74, 76, 77, 81, 103, 104
Farnese, Alessandro, 6
Feria, conde de, 33, 68, 107
Fiordibello, Antonio, 31, 85
Fisher, John, 1, 3, 96, 97
Flaminio, Marcantonio, 4, 16, 99
Flanders, 34, 108
Florence, 21
Foscarari, Egidio, 26, 27
Fowler, John, 77
Foxe, John, 33, 72, 100
Francis I, 3
Franco, Niccolò, 16, 20
Fregoso, Federico, 5

Fresneda, Bernardo, 104
Fumano, Adamo, 44

Gairdner, James, 58
Galen, 2, 95
Gardiner, Stephen, 55, 56, 73
George Plantagenet, Duke of Clarence, 1
Gheri, Filippo, 21
Giannerini, Pier Paolo, 22, 24, 76
Giberti, Antonio, 20, 31, 87
Giberti, Gian Matteo, 2, 44
Giunti, Bernardo, 92, 94
Goldwell, Thomas, 27, 31, 32, 44, 74
Gonzaga, Ercole, 27, 83
Gualteruzzi family, 30, 89
Gualteruzzi, Tommaso, 38

Harbin, George, 58
Harpsfield, Nicholas, 10, 58, 59, 102
Heidelberg, 49
Henry II, King of France, 85
Henry VII, 2
Henry VIII, 1-3
heresy, 8
Hervet, Gentian, 95
Heywood, Ellis, 10
Hill, John, 58
Holinshead, Raphael, 88
Holland, Seth, 16, 49, 53, 101
Hook, Walter Farquhar, 13-14
Hosius, Stanislaus, 38, 49-50
Hoskins, Edgar, 99

Imola, Girolamo da (Ponte, Ponzani, Pontanus), 91
Index, Congregation of the, 60
Inquisition, 4, 6, 7, 29, 39, 40, 108
Inquisition archives, 13, 14, 22, 30, 38, 49

Jeremiah, 98

Jerusalem, council of, 5
John XXIII (Angelo Roncalli,), 14
Jolliffe, Henry, 76, 77
Julius III (Giovanni Maria Ciocchi del Monte), 7, 10, 22, 75, 80, 101, 102
Lake Garda, 7
Lambeth Palace, 10
Lavaur, 94
Leonico Tomeo, Niccolò, 2
Leo the Great, Pope, 109
Leti, Gregorio, 107
Liège, 43
Lily, George, 10, 44
London, 18, 25
London synod, 1555, 9, 19, 70, 73, 91
Longueil, Christophe de, 92-93, 95-96, 105
Louvain, 77, 108
Lupset, Thomas, 93
Luther, Martin, 3, 4, 9
Lyde (or Joyner), William, 75

Machiavelli, Niccolò, 3
Machyn, Henry, 70, 72
Maffei, Bernardino, 84
Maguzzano, 7, 24
Mantova, Bendedetto da (Fontanini), 4
Manuzio, Paolo, 24, 27, 84
Marcellus II (Marcello Cervini), 10
Marcq, conference of (1555), 8
Marmion, J. P., 73, 109
Mary I, 2, 7, 8, 9, 11, 22, 55, 67, 77, 99
Mayer, Johann Friedrich, 49
Mayer, Sebald, 25, 27, 77
Mencken, Johann Burchard, 50
Merenda, Apollonio, 77, 79
Merlin, Guillaume, 109
Montmorency, Anne de, Constable of France, 24
More, Sir William, 87
More, Sir Thomas, 1, 96, 97
Morison, Richard, 53
Morone, Giovanni, 4, 6, 7, 10, 18, 19, 20, 21, 26, 31, 38, 40, 78
Muzzarelli, Girolamo, 20, 21, 22, 24, 56, 64, 85

Navagero, Bernardo, 56, 60
Navarra, Francisco de, 45
Norton, Thomas, 58

Ormanetto, Niccolò, 9, 31, 32, 82
Oxford, 2

Padua, 2, 5, 18, 92
Paleotti, Benedetto, 37
Paleotti, Gabriele, 37
Paris, 30, 109
Paris, University of, 2
Parker, Matthew, 33
Parks, George, 92
Parpaglia, Vincenzo, 31
Pate, Richard, 77
Paul, St., 5
Paul III (Alessandro Farnese), 3, 6, 82-83
Perrenot de Granvelle, Antoine, 85
Perugia, 35
Peter, St., 5
Philip II, 8, 10, 33, 55, 101
Pholio, Jacopo, 86
Pilgrimage of Grace, 3, 82
Pitts, John, 58
Pius IV (Gianangelo de' Medici), 29
Pius V (Michele Ghislieri), 29, 76
Pliny, 95
Pogson, Rex H., 58, 73
Pole, Margaret, Countess of Salisbury, 2, 4
Pole, Sir Henry, Lord Montague, 1

Index

Priuli, Alvise, 5, 16, 17, 18, 24, 26, 29, 32, 33, 35, 76, 78, 84, 86, 87
Priuli, Antonio, 87
Priuli, Matteo, 29
Pseaume, Nicholas, 106
Pye, Benjamin, 14
Pyning, Henry, 16, 32, 34, 76, 77, 109

Querini, Angelo Maria, 13, 42, 49, 52
Quistri, Deodato, 21, 31
Quistri, Philomeno, 21

Rastell, John, 77
Ravesteyn, Josse (Jodochus Tiletanus or Diletanus), 25
Rebiba, Scipione, 29
Regensburg, Colloquy of, 1541, 5
Ridley, Jaspar, 56
Rome, 7, 10, 20, 24, 29
Rullo, Donato, 18, 19, 54, 56

Sadoleto, Jacopo, 2
Sander, Nicholas, 48, 77
Sandro, Bernardino, 43, 44
Santa Croce, Prospero, 47
Sant' Erculano, College of (Barnabites), Perugia, 35-36
Sarum, Use of, 99
Savonarola, Girolamo, 24
Schelhorn, Johann Georg, 49, 50
Scotti, Bernardino, 24, 74, 89
Selden, John, 58
Selve, Georges de, 94
Seripando, Girolamo, 18, 19, 20, 26, 27, 38, 60, 61, 83, 84
Seymour, Edward, Duke of Somerset, 55
Solomon, 101
Soranzo, Jacopo, 86

Soto, Pedro de, 108
Spain, 108
Starkey, Thomas, 95
St. John of Jerusalem, Knights of, 70
St. Mary-Arches, London, 69
Strype, John, 33, 70, 72, 88

Tanner, Thomas, 12, 13, 14, 42
Tapper, Ruard, 25, 108
Testamentum vere christianum, 25
Thynne, Francis, 101
Tootell, Hugh (pseudonym: Charles Dodd), 12, 42, 76
Torelli, Lelio, 21
Trent, Council of, 4, 5, 26-27, 38
Tresham, Sir Thomas, 70, 72
Truchsess, Otto, 25, 47, 48, 77

Ugalde, Juan, 87

Valdés, Juan de, 4
Valier, Agostino, 59
Venice, 2, 4, 18, 27, 29
Vergerio, Pier Paolo, 25, 47, 48
Vergil, Polydore, 82
Verhasselt, Martin, 25
Villagarcia, Juan de, 104
Villeneuve, Simon de, 94
Viterbo, 4, 48
Vittori, Mariano, 31

Wayland, John, 99
Wood, Anthony à, 42, 105
Worcester, 77

York, Archbishopric of, 2

Zeno, Apostolo, 84
Zimmermann, Athanasius, 13
Zürich, 49

www.ingramcontent.com/pod-product-compliance
Lightning Source LLC
Chambersburg PA
CBHW080801020526
44114CB00035B/5